BREEZY
and
DODO
A life story

WITH LOVE

John

By:
John "Breezy" F. Bartkowski
2014

Copyright

ACKNOWLEDGEMENT

This has not been a solo effort by any means. The story is a compilation of my recollections, family records, and stories told to me by my parents and others. My sister-in-law, Belle Kassib, and my siblings, Lorraine and Gene, confirmed many of my recollections and offered their own that I've included. My daughter Janet Raines has devoted countless hours to typing my scribbled writing. Daughter Diane Niemkiewicz has helped in the editing phase.

Lorraine and my friend Kitty helped me to gather historical data from Dickson City Borough and St. Mary's Parish records, Corpus Christi Parish in Glen Lyon, and from tombstones at associated cemeteries.

It was quite an experience visiting the cemeteries. We located tombstones with family names, and I saw the names of ones that I had known and visited as a youngster so many years ago. I recalled the hardships that they faced and overcame with hard work and determination and the events that affected their lives, some good or bad, some funny or sad, and offered a prayer for their souls.

I extend a sincere "Thank you" to my helpers. Let the story begin. Once upon a time, oops, wrong story.

INTRODUCTION

"Hi, I'm Breezy, and this is my wife, Dodo." With hand extended, that was how I usually introduced us to new acquaintances. They would react with a smile, a look of disbelief, and a series of questions – "How and when did you get those names?" – "How did you two meet and marry?" – etc.

Our response was quite simple. We were born a week apart in December 1928 to couples who were friends, in Dickson City, Pennsylvania. I was given my nickname by a nun in elementary school, at about the same time that Dodo was given hers by her brother Ted. We first met and became friends in 9th grade, and our friendship grew during our high school years. We began dating while attending local colleges, and, a few years later, in October 1950, at the age of 21, were married in the same church in which we had been baptized.

This response would lead to more questions. Over the years, our three daughters, Donna, Diane, and Janet, asked similar and many more questions. We answered them with the full extent of our recollections. Yet, it seemed that there was always another question.

Now, in my golden years, my daughters have persuaded me to tell them, and their children, the full story of "Breezy" and "Dodo," including the histories of our families and the town where we were born and raised.

I offer this story to my daughters with love from Dad, and it is my fervent hope that one day they will add their stories for future generations to peruse.

Breezy

Breezy's Family

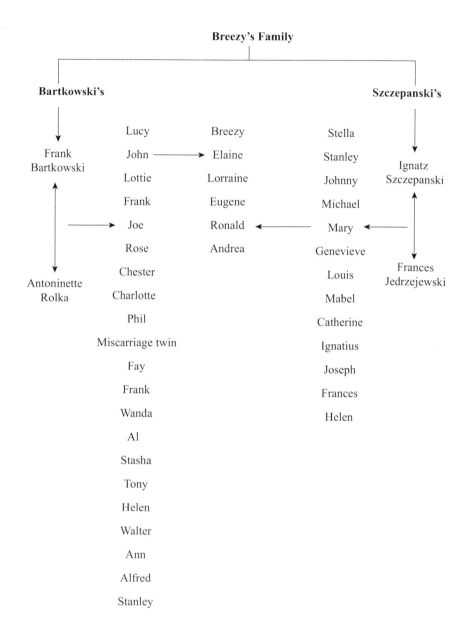

Bartkowski's			Szczepanski's

	Lucy	Breezy	Stella
Frank Bartkowski	John →	Elaine	Stanley
	Lottie	Lorraine	Johnny
	Frank	Eugene	Michael
→	Joe	Ronald ←	Mary ←
	Rose	Andrea	Genevieve
	Chester		Louis
Antoninette Rolka	Charlotte		Mabel
	Phil		Catherine
	Miscarriage twin		Ignatius
	Fay		Joseph
	Frank		Frances
	Wanda		Helen
	Al		
	Stasha		
	Tony		
	Helen		
	Walter		
	Ann		
	Alfred		
	Stanley		

Ignatz Szczepanski

Frances Jedrzejewski

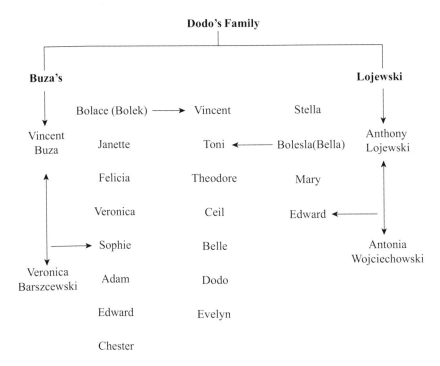

Dodo's Family

Buza's

Vincent Buza

Bolace (Bolek) → Vincent

Janette

Toni ← Bolesla(Bella)

Felicia

Theodore

Veronica

Ceil

Sophie

Belle

Veronica Barszcewski

Adam

Dodo

Edward

Evelyn

Chester

Lojewski

Stella

Anthony Lojewski

Mary

Edward ←

Antonia Wojciechowski

Table of Contents

CHAPTER ONE
THE TOWN

The area in northeast Pennsylvania incorporated as the Borough of Dickson City is located on the western bank of the Lackawanna River, in the valley and county of the same name. To the north, it borders the Borough of Blakely. To the south, it borders a section of the city of Scranton, the largest and most populated city in the area, which serves as the county seat and the transportation, civic, and business hub.

The area saw its first white settlers in 1786, with Timothy Steven's family arriving from Westchester, New York. Eleven years later, the Vaughan and Potter families arrived, and a year after that, so did the brothers Decker. Shortly thereafter, a few more settlers arrived. These early settlers built cabins, cleared and farmed the land, and supplemented their farm products with fish they caught in the river and the abundant wild game that they hunted.

In the early part of the 19th century, T. Stevens became the area's first industrialist when he built a sawmill on the bank of the river, cut and processed local timber, and rafted it downriver to Scranton, then known as Slocum Hollow.

More settlers arrived, bearing such names as Snyder, Dickson (whom the town would be named after), Pugh, Baker, and Jones. Other settlers bore the names Jermyn, Throop, Pancoast, and Price, the latter three buying parcels of land from the brothers Decker. The Price parcel was soon called Priceburg. Some of the new settlers arrived from Germany, while others came from English-speaking western European countries that included Scots, Welsh, English, and Irish, the latter fleeing the potato famine in Ireland.

By the middle of the century, rich deposits of anthracite coal, a hard, clean, and long-burning source of heat, were being discovered in nearby settlements that dotted both sides of the river. Mining operations were underway as rail lines were being laid and canals dug to transport the coal to the large city markets. This "hard" coal, when used as a heat source, particularly in steam engines, emitted a white smoke in contrast to the cinder-laden black smoke emitted by the "soft" bituminous coal.

Coal mining began in the Borough in 1859, when a settler named Chittendon found coal as he opened a drift in the western hillside. Later, he sank a shaft at a lower level and erected a breaker and dwellings to house his employees. The next year, another individual opened a similar operation but also erected a company store where his employees purchased their home- and work-related items. The opening of the mine operations prompted the arrival of more immigrants, many of Irish descent. Their influence in the community is evident in the names of the Borough's early politicians and educators.

In 1875, the year the Borough was incorporated, the first elections were held to select a burgess, town council, school board, and the first chief of police. Fifteen years later, the first ordinance was passed; the Borough began receiving electrical power and street lights from a nearby community power company, and a volunteer fire company was organized.

By 1880, the Borough had at least one operating mine and breaker in each of its three wards as the Johnson shaft was sunk, its associated breaker and company homes were erected, and the Miles slope, where Dad and his brothers eventually worked, began operating.

The Miles slope and a few adjacent community mines were owned by the Hudson Coal Co., probably the largest company in the area. The mine outputs were processed at the centrally-located "Eddy Creek" breaker; arguably the largest in the state. Eddy Creek employed several thousand workers during the peak coal mining boom era, and it was where eventually, as a teenager, I worked one summer.

The new mines served as magnets and attracted immigrants from non-English speaking European countries that included Russians, Slovaks and primarily Poles. The latter, in a couple of decades, became the largest ethnic group in the Borough and exerted their influence in the political arena as officials were elected bearing names such as Nowakowski, Dembowski, Buza, and Bartkowski. From a population of about 800 residents in the late 1800s, the population grew to an estimated peak of 14,000 in the late 1930s, with the largest increase occurring between 1900 and 1920.

* * * * *

The settlers harbored deep religious beliefs and a determination to establish a formal education system. In 1883, the Primitive Methodist was the first church built. Five years later, St. Thomas, the first Catholic church in the Borough, was built and was later referred to as the "Irish" church.

In 1892, St. Mary's Polish Roman Catholic church was established with the arrival of a resident pastor. The newly-built church was a wooden, two-level structure with a seating capacity of 200. It was where Dodo's dad would soon serve as an altar boy. The influx of more Polish immigrants soon exceeded the church's capacity, and in late 1911, on an adjoining property, a new, large, twin bell towered, cathedral style church was dedicated, with approximately five times greater seating capacity. Eventually, our parents were married in the new church, and it was where Dodo and I would be baptized, receive first Holy Communion, and be confirmed; where I would serve as an altar boy, and where we would be married.

Four more churches of various denominations and a synagogue were eventually erected to serve the immigrants.

At the time of the incorporation (1875), there were three two-room schoolhouses. Eventually, there would be at least one public elementary school in each of the wards, each housing grades 1 through 6, and known by such names as Columbus, Washington, Lafayette, Lincoln, etc. Later, a middle/jr. high school was erected and housed grades 7 through 9. The senior high school housed grades 10 through 12.

St. Mary's Parochial Elementary School supplemented the public schools and was initiated in 1892 in the basement of the original church. Several lay teachers assembled and taught the students in three group levels, since there were no classrooms. This teaching and learning environment continued for the next nineteen years. As religious activities began being held in the new church in 1911, and as student enrollment was increasing, the entire old church was converted into a school facility with classrooms. Over the next fourteen years, the enrollment increased and a small contingent of Bernadine nuns arrived to staff the school.

In 1925, the nearby, newly-constructed, modern, three-level parish school was first occupied. It contained sixteen classrooms, housing grades 1 through 8, with a student capacity of about 1,000. The school was completely staffed by a complement of about 19 Bernadine nuns who took up residence across the street in a convent on parish grounds.

The building also contained a hall with a quality wooden dance floor that also served as the basketball court, a stage adorned with velvet drapes that matched those covering side windows; backstage stairway access to lower and upper level dressing and staging areas; a balcony with a projection booth with a multi-colored light projector; and a kitchen and beverage dispensing facilities. The school building, constructed at a cost of $225,000, also became the civic, social, and athletic center for the parish.

* * * * *

The coal companies in general and the Hudson Coal Company in particular employed the largest portion of the area's work force as their employees numbered in the thousands. The company's operations consisted of the underground mining activity and the aboveground facilities to process and transport the coal to market.

The mining of the coal was accomplished by crews of 3 or 4 men led by a state certified miner who had completed courses in mining operations, safety, and the use of dynamite. He was paid per ton of coal mined, while his crew was paid a daily rate.

Mining coal was a physically demanding job performed in a dusty and dangerous environment, with the only illumination coming from the open flame carbide lamps attached to the men's caps. Quite often, the men worked in a stooped position and, occasionally, on their knees.

There were several dangers that the men faced. They erected timbers and cross beams to shore up and support the roof and left natural coal support pillars in the large chamber work areas. Nevertheless, roof collapses occasionally occurred, and they were usually preceded by overhead cracking sounds. Many men escaped in time while some were caught under the collapse and were seriously injured or killed. Dad's brother, my godfather, Uncle Chet, was seriously injured in one, and Mom's Uncle John and our next door neighbor were killed, all on separate occasions in different mines.

Although the mines were ventilated to a degree, pockets of a relatively odorless mine gas occasionally formed, particularly in work areas. Canaries, vulnerable to minimal gas levels, were housed in the mine, and the sight of suddenly dying birds was a warning signal for the men to immediately vacate the area. It wasn't a fool-proof system, and on occasion, as men entered a chamber, explosions occurred, ignited by the men's open flame lamps. Some men survived serious and painful burns, while some, like Mom's younger brother Louie, suffered a painful death. In later years, bulb lamps powered by battery packs were introduced and reduced the number of mine explosions.

There were also other types of mine accidents that resulted in severe injuries or death. The worst occurred in 1911 in a mine in the adjacent town of Throop. Seventy-two men died of suffocation as they were trapped in a section of the mine by a fire that began in and destroyed the underground engine room. Fifteen of the men were from St. Mary's Parish.

The men injured in the various accidents received on-site first aid treatment. The severely injured were transported to hospitals, or along with the bodies of the dead men, clad in their work clothes and sprinkled with the coal dust, were transported to and deposited at the family home for additional care or burial.

Mules were an integral part of the coal mining activity. They and their provisions were housed in a makeshift stable in the mine and on the surface, a more elaborate facility including a barn. In both locations, they were led by mostly young "mule drivers" as they hauled the low silhouette mine cars on narrow gauge rails through the various mining and processing activities. The mules were a valuable asset and, more so than the men, were well fed and medically tended to. Eventually, they were replaced in the mine by electric motors controlled by "motormen" and above ground by "lokies," a local term defining the miniature steam locomotives, whose movements throughout the area were marked by the blaring of their high pitched shrieking whistle.

In the breaker, the coal was crushed by heavy duty equipment into various sizes, including the popular sizes of chestnut, pea, or rice. The sizes were separated as they were sifted while passing over the various hole-sized shaker grates. The coal, along with seemingly constant dripping water, flowed down the chutes to eventually fill the large railroad cars and local delivery trucks.

It was along the chutes of flowing coal and undesirable slate that lads as young as 8 or 9 years of age spent the entire work day hunched over the chutes, picking out the slate. It was diverted to the dumps that eventually covered acres and reached heights of 50 feet or more. For some, like Dad, it was the first step in a 40-plus year mining career. For others, like Dodo's Uncle Ed Mako, it was a shorter career as their lives were curtailed by the "black lung" disease. And yet for others, like Dodo's dad, it was a short career as they soon successfully ventured into other occupations

During the coal mining era, the men occasionally went "on strike" and received concessions from the companies.

These concessions included higher wages, a work week reduced to five days, and a work day reduced to 8 hours. The men became unionized as they joined the United Mine Workers led by John Mitchell and his successor, John L. Lewis. Both men were revered by the workers. The Holy Trinity hanging on a wall in our home included a picture of the Sacred Heart flanked by photos of the Pope and John L. Lewis.

Some of the strikes were of short duration and settled without incident, but the one in the early 1930s was a lengthy one and included violence and damage to coal company property. Dad's cousin Dudu and Mom's older brother Johnny were convicted for participating in causing this damage when they dynamited a company storage shed. Johnny lost the finger tips on one hand, and during their incarceration, the Feds initiated action to deport him to his native Poland. Dad, in a politically influential position as Town Council President, in concert with our highly respected and influential congressman, Pat Boland, met with President Franklin D. Roosevelt and was successful in convincing the President to halt the deportation activity. Congressman Boland had access to the President in his position as the Majority Whip in the Democrat-controlled House of Representatives. As such, he was very effective in corralling the votes required to pass the President's legislative agenda.

As a young lad, I accompanied Dad on his follow-up trip to the central Pennsylvania Federal Penitentiary to visit and update Uncle Johnny. It was a frightening experience as I heard the loud clang of the heavy metal door that closed behind us as we entered the visitor area. Dad used the opportunity to point out the possible fate that awaited people who broke the law. But soon, I was sharing Uncle Johnny's joy as Dad informed him of the good news emanating from the meeting with the President. Uncle Johnny was soon released, and his gratitude and the mutual respect he and Dad had for each other was forever cemented.

* * * * *

As the population expanded in the early 1900s, so did other occupational venues and business activity. The men had occupational opportunities at the manufacturing and steel fabricating facility, or at two foundries, one of which produced the castings that were used in the production of a top quality coal stove. Construction tradesmen were steadily employed as new homes and buildings were being constructed.

The women, especially the young single ones, obtained employment at the various silk mills and garment producing facilities that dotted the borough landscape. Our moms and their younger sisters developed excellent seamstress skills and made some of their own patterned garments.

They went on to extend their skills and patterned, marked, and hand-sewed decorative quilts.

The business community expanded, and the vast majority of the establishments were family owned and operated small businesses. They included multiple banks, pharmacies, hardware stores, bakeries, and neighborhood barber shops. The latter were usually patronized by the older male family members, as the youngsters had their hair cut while perched on a chair in their home basement or on the back porch, adorned by a guide bowl, by a family member using seemingly dull scissors, and equally dull hand-operated clippers.

Doctors made house calls, and the owners of the coal and ice house, the soda bottling works and the dairy provided home delivery; the latter on a daily basis. The baked goods salesmen drove through the neighborhood on a daily basis and announced their arrival with horn toots while groups of customers selected and purchased their favorite doughnuts, pies, and rye bread. There were other businesses in town that provided various services, including a diner, blacksmith, jeweler, and shoe sales and repair facilities.

The most numerous and widespread businesses were the grocery stores and taverns that usually occupied part of, or the entire first floor of, the family residence. The grocery stores were located along the main streets and in many of the residential neighborhoods, and it was not unusual to find one at each end of the block and one in the middle. The taverns were primarily located along the main streets, though a smattering of them were also in the neighborhoods.

Some of the grocers only offered the basic food staples, while the larger establishments offered an array of fresh vegetables, poultry, and cuts of beef and pork. Young family members or neighbor lads used their wagons to deliver the customers' larger weekend orders.

At least a half dozen grocers made and claimed that their smoked kielbasa was the best in the area. The claim was also touted by their customer base and out-of-town patrons, and was a topic of discussion at family gatherings and food festivals. We had a couple of these outlets and a bakery in our neighborhood, and when the kielbasa orders spiked for an upcoming holiday, we were treated to the aroma of kielbasa being smoked and hot bread being removed from the ovens. A Polish delight.

* * * * *

During the peak population era in the late 1930s, there were 36 taverns in operation. Some residents referred to them as inns or bars, while older immigrants called them beer gardens. Some residents, especially during the Depression, preferred or could only afford to stay at home and partake in the cheaper, yet potent, homemade "hooch."

(One summer, while attending elementary school, I would occasionally ride along in the truck with Mom's brother Uncle "Iggy" as he delivered sacks of feed and grain for our local distributor. On one such occasion, at a home in town, he delivered a sack of grain and another and another and finally a fourth. My curiosity was piqued, and I asked him why he was making such a big drop at a home where I could only see chickens roaming the backyard. Smiling, he responded, "She's an elderly woman and likes her chickens well fed and plump." Sounded good to me.

Years later, as we were reminiscing, I mentioned that lady and the incident. "I remember her well," he said. "It was the middle of the Depression; her husband had difficulty finding steady work, and she was earning some money by making and selling the best "moonshine" in the town. The Feds heard rumors of her activity and occasionally had an agent on stake out, watching for customers and how she was disposing of the residue. Finally, on one stake out, the agent noted that the chickens were cackling louder and acting more erratically than usual. Upon further observation, he noted that the chickens were actually staggering and realized that she was feeding the residue to the chickens. The Feds issued her a warning and she stopped the operation, to the disappointment of her customers.)

Some of the establishments attracted couples, because they earned a reputation for the lunches and dinners they offered in a congenial atmosphere. A few establishments were renowned for the late summer family clambakes they sponsored. These were all-day events that were held in a farm pasture and featured hot dogs, kielbasa, salads, fresh-picked corn on the cob, and steamed clams. Beer flowed freely from the tap, as did birch and root beers. The men played softball games, and the youngsters joined in or played in their own games, to the mothers' refrains of "Watch out for the cow flop." When the refrains went unheeded, the aftermath clean-up was accomplished in the stream that flowed through the pasture.

Coal mining and politics dominated the conversations at various establishments. However, at the renamed Blackhawk Bar, a tribute to the high school mascot, local and national sports activities dominated the conversations. The owner sponsored local athletic teams, and his client base included sports enthusiasts and active and retired athletes, some with legendary resumes.

The Town House Tavern, locally referred to as Johnny Hot Dogs, a nickname the owner acquired while previously operating a small eatery that featured hot dogs, was one of a few establishments not located in a family residence. It was in a high ceilinged former bank building and contained an oval bar, plush booths, a small dance area, and a mezzanine for private parties and dinners. Excellent food was served, and it attracted couples, but it also had a steady daily patron base of at least a half dozen men. With the daily newspaper in hand, they seemed engrossed in reading the local and national news. In fact, they were analyzing the horse racing page to determine their selection in the afternoon races being run at various tracks. As post time approached, they would scurry to the several pay phone booths to place their bets.

The state blue laws required that all bars be closed on Sundays, and, by all outward appearances, they were. The windows were shuttered and the cash register drawer was constantly open, but the exhaust fans were operating, and the patrons gained entrance by ringing the back door bell. State agents occasionally conducted raids to snare violators. However, the owners would be alerted to the imminent raids by a curtly coded phone message and promptly close the facility as the patrons vacated the premises.

* * * * *

The residents also had access to other social and entertainment activities at the theater, church festivals, and socials, and the dances and picnics held at the St. Mary's Parish-owned Polonia Park. For those seeking more varied occupational opportunities or more extensive shopping and entertainment options, it was about a half-hour bus or trolley ride to downtown Scranton.

CHAPTER TWO
OUR FAMILIES

BUZA/LOJEWSKI (Dodo's)

On December 22, 1889, in the Village of Bladkowicz, in Russian-controlled Poland, Vincent and Veronica Barszcewski Buza were blessed with the birth of their first child, a son. They named him Bolace, and he would be called Bolek. When Bolek was 3 years old, he and his mom and dad, ages 20 and 25 respectively, migrated to the town of Dickson City in northeastern Pennsylvania.

They were in the early wave of Eastern European, Polish-speaking people who were arriving in an area that was mostly populated by English-speaking, Western European immigrants who had arrived earlier.

The influx of immigrants, particularly from Poland, was occurring at a rapidly increasing rate. The new immigrants were primarily young couples, and many were accompanied by young children, including infants. They departed a Poland, where many of the men worked in the coal mines, that were under either German or Russian control and where they were being subjected to political and religious suppression. They, as well as their predecessors, were lured to the Dickson City area by industry ads that were published in European newspapers, extolling the area's virtues and job opportunities in the expanding coal mining and textile industries. Some were enticed by glowing letters from family members or friends who preceded them.

Vincent and Veronica settled into a home in the 600 block of Carmalt Street, and Vincent, who was a coal miner in Poland, went to work at a local coal mine. He soon became a certified miner and eventually was promoted to a mine supervisory position. The coal company rewarded his work ethic by naming a coal vein in his honor.

* * * * *

The family joined other Polish families as congregation members at St. Mary's Roman Catholic Polish church. The church was the religious, educational, and cultural hub for the immigrants.

Bolace enrolled in and attended the church basement school for several years, where he received a religious and Polish heritage education while simultaneously learning how to read, write, and properly speak Polish and the new English language. He was an eager student; he learned all of the educational facets well and became an altar boy at the age of 6. He became proficient in math and the adaptation of the English language to the point that his rapidly expanding circle of English speaking neighborhood friends quickly accepted him and began calling him Billy. These attributes would serve him well in the future.

At about the age of 8 or 9, he, as did many other young boys of similar age, dropped out of school and began working as a "breaker boy" slate picker at a local mine in order to contribute to the family finances. He worked at the breaker 10 to 12 hours per day, 5 or 6 days a week, hunched over the chutes, picking out the slate with cut, bruised, and painful fingers---all for wages amounting to a few pennies an hour.

As the coal operations resumed following the 1900 strike, Bill's dad dissuaded him from returning to work in the coal operations and particularly in any job down in the mine. Billy spent his teen years working at non-mining activities, particularly in the business arena. At the end of his teens he was tending bar at a local establishment and harboring a desire to own a business.

* * * * *

The family was growing in size as he was joined by seven siblings. The sisters included Janette, twins Felicia and Veronica, and Sophie, (the twins died days apart, at an early age, from injuries they received as a rocking chair they were exuberantly sharing overturned). The brothers included Adam, Edward, and Chester. Eventually, Adam was appointed to the town police force, where he and his partner, Tony Zalewski (who would be DoDo's godfather), became renowned for their ability to break up floating crap games. Their technique was quite simple; they would join in the game and win most of the money. Soon, games in progress were disbanded at the approach of the partners. Edward went on to attend and graduate from Penn State with a business degree, and Chester became an outstanding athlete in high school.

* * * * *

The large influx of Polish immigrants soon inundated the 200 seat capacity of their church, and, in 1909, the construction plans for the new, much larger church were approved by the pastor and the church committee.

Billy was an active parish fund raiser and, as part of his bartending activities, he solicited donations from the patrons to help defray some of the new church construction costs. He also joined his and other societies' members as they went on foot, soliciting donations from locals and residents in other communities.

On November 26, 1911, the month before Billy's 22nd birthday, the new, large, cathedral-style church was dedicated. The old, two-story church building was retained as an expanded educational facility, as a meeting place for the new societies that were being organized, and as the site of their fund raising socials and dances.

Billy attended and participated in the various events. It was at one of them that he met and began socializing with Bella Lojewski, a young, pretty, new parishioner whose family had moved into his neighborhood upon their recent arrival from Glen Lyon, PA.

* * * * *

Anthony Lojewski and Antonia Wojciechowski, as teenagers, migrated to northeastern Pennsylvania. They arrived separately from a farm area in German-controlled Poland, where they were born and raised, and she had worked on a farm. On July 7, 1892, they were married in St. Adalbert Roman Catholic Church in Glen Lyon, Pennsylvania, and on February 17, 1895, were blessed with the birth of their second child, a daughter they named Bolesla and who would soon be called Bella.

Following their marriage, Bella's parents bought and, utilizing her mother's skills, farmed an area of land between town and an outlying area called the "Patch." There they also began growing the family. Bella was preceded in birth by her sister, Stella, and followed by siblings Mary and Edward and some other children who did not survive birth or early infancy. As the children grew, they attended a limited elementary school for a few years and helped work on the farm or in local textile mills.

* * * * *

It was circa 1910, when Bella was in her mid-teens, that her parents sold the farm and moved the family some 40 miles north, to Dickson City. It was much larger and more populated, with a sizable Polish immigrant population and expanded occupational opportunities. They bought a three-story building on the corner of Price and Walker streets that contained a tavern on the basement level, family residence on the second, and apartments that they rented to newly arrived immigrants on the third. Upon their arrival, the family joined St. Mary's parish.

In the next decade or so, as the daughters were getting married and beginning to raise their own young families, Bella's parents sold their building and moved into a duplex a few blocks away that they shared with their oldest daughter, Stella ,and her young family. Soon thereafter, they bought a 25+ acre farm in the community of Hopbottom, some 30 miles north.

Bella's mother was a very short woman with a big, warm heart. She was energetic, with a subtle determination and a strong mind of her own. She would undertake and complete any task that she set her mind to. Drawing on her childhood experiences, she and her young adult son,

Eddie, along with a hired hand, operated the farm. They grew vegetables, mowed and stacked hay, raised chickens, pigs, and turkeys, milked their cows, and tended to a couple of work horses.

The farm also contained a small but rich quarry of top grade slate stone. They sold the slate to various builders, the milk to a co-op, and the other wares at the community market, and they changed the family name to Lewis. Throughout the community and within her circle of grandchildren and younger friends, Antoinette was affectionately called and referred to as "Grandma Lewis."

She loved having her grandchildren spend a few weeks at the farm each summer, helping with the chores, and, in turn, they enjoyed the experience. After feeding and cleaning up after the animals, collecting eggs, and stacking hay, they would learn how to milk cows and ride the horses. In a shallow pond across the road, they would swim and catch fish and frogs that Grandma would prepare.

The youngsters most enjoyed their interchange with, and the entertainment provided by, Uncle Eddie. He was an affable, hard working, strong young man and also an excellent self-taught musician. They would test his strength as they took turns hanging on his outstretched arms and were in awe as he put on a display of flexing his arm muscles. In the evenings, as they relaxed in the parlor, he would tell told them various stories and lead them in singalongs as he played the piano, mouth organ, or banjo. Eddie had his own music group and entertained at events in various surrounding farm communities, including the town of Montrose, the county seat.

* * * * *

Bella, along with working at a silk mill, helped prepare food that was served in the family tavern and became an active parishioner. She joined the Dzieci Marji (Children of Mary) Society and helped to organize and participate in their sponsored fund raising social events. It was at one of these events that she met Billy Buza. He made quite an impression on her, and she reportedly told her girlfriend that he was the man she would marry.

Her foresight was correct, as their relationship soon blossomed into a romance. On November 8, 1914, Bella, age 19, and Billy, age 24, were married in the new St. Mary's Church. They bought a combination residence and tavern at the main intersection in town. Billy had his own tavern business, and Bella prepared the food that they served.

In August 1915, they were blessed with the birth of their first child, a son they named Vincent. He was followed in basically two year intervals by Antoinette (Toni), Theodore (Ted), and Ceil. Their property was ill suited for the youngsters to play in or for Bella to grow gardens.

In 1923, as they were blessed with the birth of their fifth child, a daughter they named Belle, they relocated to a newly constructed two story building a few homes away, at 512 Storrs Avenue.

The new, spacious, two-story building, containing all indoor amenities including central heat, was situated on a property with an adequate back yard to accommodate gardens and child play. Half of the first level contained family activity rooms while the other half contained the tavern with an attached dining room, where Bella's prepared food was served. On the second level, along with bedrooms, it also contained a back room with direct stairway access and dumbwaiter service to the tavern dining area. Bella used the room to host small social gatherings with friends and group quilting activities. Billy used the room to host meetings with political colleagues.

Bella and Billy continued to participate in parish activities, and Billy also continued an equivalent interest in the rapidly expanding community growth and the related politics. A few years earlier, at the urging of his Polish and English speaking client base, he ran for and was overwhelmingly elected to a seat on the nine member city council. He was later re-elected to several 4-year terms. During his tenure on the council, more streets were paved and, more notably, a bridge was built spanning the Lackawanna River to the neighboring town of Lower

Throop. The bridge provided an alternate route to the city of Scranton.

During the spring of 1928, Bella became aware that she was again with child.

BARTKOWSKI/SZCZEPANSKI (Breezy's)

Frank and Antoinette Rolka Bartkowski were born, raised, and married in the town of Jablonowa, in a section of Poland that was under Germany's control. Frank was born in 1881. At a young age, he was an orphan and an unhappy child. He was thereafter shuffled among relatives. Antoinette was born in 1884 and was raised and worked on a tenant farm. (Later in life, Grandma enjoyed telling a story about her tall, husky, and strong father, who was reputed to often generate and loudly expel gas – "fartski." He used that asset to teach her, and the other young children, to count. In the early morning hours, as he led them in single file to work in the fields, he would begin expelling, and they would laugh and shout in unison, "jeden" (one)... "dwa" (two)... "trzy" (three)...etc.).

Frank and Antoinette were married in 1900 when he was 19 and she was 16. In March 1902, they were blessed with the birth of their first child, a daughter they named Lucy. Following the baby's birth, Frank migrated to Dickson City, where he joined his wife's brother and sister, who were in residence there, and obtained a job in a coal mine.

Later that year, Antoinette and baby Lucy rejoined Frank in their new country. They soon bought and moved into a coal company-built duplex at 1022/24 Carmalt Street, where they occupied one half of the duplex, rented out the other half, and took in temporary boarders who slept in two basement rooms. Each half contained a kitchen, parlor, and two upstairs bedrooms. Neither side had any closets or bathrooms. The amenities were limited and included a sink, cold tap water, a coal stove for cooking and heating, and a duplex outhouse.

It was in that home on March 3, 1904, that they were blessed with the birth of their second child, a son they named John. Considering that child birth is a blessing from God, Frank and Antoinette surely were an extremely blessed couple, for in the next 21 years she was with child 13 more times and delivered 19 more babies, including four sets of twins and a set of triplets. In one 30-month period, she delivered two sets of twins and a set of triplets, but only one baby of each multiple birth survived beyond infancy. All in all, fourteen children, 7 sons and 7 daughters, lived well into their adult years.

When John was 8 years old and finishing second grade, he had to drop out of school and go to work to financially help the family, for by then there were 6 younger siblings that needed to be fed and clothed. John got a job as a breaker boy at the local coal company, where he picked the slate out of the flowing coal (ala Bill Buza, but a decade or more later). This was the beginning of what was to be his 40 plus-year career in the coal mines. He soon went into the mine as a laborer and subsequently studied for and passed the state test and was awarded a miner certificate. (Dad later told me that, while working as a young slate picker, the noise from the flowing coal and nearby heavy machinery made oral communication virtually impossible. Young lads needing a relief break would signal the foreman by flicking a finger across the nose. He would respond in kind and nod approval.)

As more babies were born, brothers Joe, Chet, and Phil dropped out of elementary school and joined John and their father in the coal mine.

* * * * *

The decade of the 20s saw a significant change in the family's activities and growth. Babies were still being born, and the oldest children were reaching adulthood. The oldest boys, as would their younger male siblings, were growing to heights of 6 feet or more and weighing around 200 lbs. John was the tallest, at a muscle-hardened height of 6'5" and a weight in the 225 lb range.

The family eventually moved into their newly constructed dwelling at 1041 Carmalt Street, while retaining their old house as a duplex rental property. The new dwelling had all indoor amenities, including a central steam heat system fueled by a large, coal-fired furnace that was located in a sizeable basement. The basement also included an area where the boys stored and set up their physical conditioning and sports equipment and developed and honed their skills.

The new dwelling was more than large enough to comfortably accommodate the large family. In an area on the first level they furnished and opened a grocery store that was run by Antoinette, with the help of the children. Half of the second floor was easily converted into a four room apartment that they could rent to any of their children who were approaching marriageable age.

They continued their routine of raising chickens as an egg and food supply; grazed a cow that provided milk for the family, particularly the younger children, and raised a couple of pigs each year. With the help of his sons and neighbors, Frank slaughtered and butchered the pigs, and much of the meat was consumed by the family. The rest, including the intestines that were used as casing, was made into fresh and smoked kielbasi that they featured in the store, along with their homemade kishka. Nothing was wasted, as the animal waste was used to fertilize their flower and vegetable gardens.

* * * * *

As John turned 20 in 1924, he was increasingly interested and active in the parish and community political activities while furthering his education by attending night classes at various locations, including St. Thomas College in nearby Scranton. He joined the men's St. Stanislaus Kostka Society, a group that recommended various parish activities and was a major fund raising organization. By the age of 24, he was appointed to the church committee that, along with the pastor, approved the construction and funding of various parish projects. In a few years, he was elected to the town council, where he would serve several terms, including some time as Council President.

It was during this era of parish activity involvement that John served as the ticket sales chairman for a parish outing. The promotion advised, "If you can jump over John, you get in free." It was also during these activities that he became acquainted with his 14-year senior, Bill Buza.

* * * * *

In the late 1920s, shortly after the new elementary school and its centerpiece hall were built, a young adult male basketball team was formed, with the approval and blessing of Monsignor Szpotanski, to compete against valley parish and athletic club teams.

In that era, the games were played on a court that was enclosed by heavy netting hung from the ceiling to the floor. There weren't any out of bounds; a player could stop and restart dribbling, and the two-handed set shot was the vogue. Ball possession at the start of the game, and each score thereafter, was decided by the center's jump ball at midcourt.

John, now known as "Big Bart," had organized basketball team experience, including a year at St. Thomas College, and several years in the professional NEP (Northeastern PA) League for the down valley town of Pittston. He joined the team, along with brothers Chet, Phil, and Al. With their heights and muscular weights, along with their strong, competitive natures, which had grown during their own backyard competitive games, they were a formidable group. They made up the bulk of the starting lineup. They soon were referred to collectively as the Bart Brothers and individually as "Big Bart," "C. Bart," "P. Bart," and "A. Bart."

The dedicated and highly competitive new team was an immediate success and went undefeated for quite a number of consecutive years. During the initial 13 years, the team reportedly lost only 2 games. As their wins continued, tales of their legendary accomplishments spread throughout the area and were being reported in the valley newspapers. They were targeted as the team to beat and were playing in front of standing room only crowds at home and away. Soon, discussions in sport circles inextricably linked St. Mary's and the Bart Brothers.

Monsignor, who was the honorary coach, subtly reveled in the team's success, and at home games was joined on the team bench by Dr. Gumbar, the team physician. With his height, John handled the center jump ball and controlled the backboards, while his brothers, all good two-handed set shooters, did the bulk of the scoring. Phil and Al were exceptional, some referred to them as classy ball handlers, and shot mostly from the perimeter as they faked and outmaneuvered their opponents. Chet enjoyed playing the inside physical game and used his solid bulk and aggressiveness to drive through opponents for layups. This led to some brief altercations, some of which required the doctor to stitch a wound or break out the smelling salts.

A more serious altercation turned into a team brawl at an away game. Police responded to quell it and control the crowd, some of whom were trying to claw through the nets to join the fray. After the game, the concerned police chief provided Monsignor and the team a courteous, safe escort to the town boundary. Chet used these experiences, along with others gained in sparring bouts with Phil, to attempt what turned out to be a short and not too successful pro-boxing career. He retired after losing his first fight to a bigger veteran pro boxer. Chet went all-out during this match, to the point that while in the ring between rounds, he had to replace his split boxing shorts while shielded by men holding round number placards.

In a few years, as the game rules were changing, the Bart Brothers began retiring and putting an end to their era. (As a youngster, I was fortunate enough to have attended some of their later stage games. It was there that I first nurtured a dream that I would grow up and be good enough to play on the St. Mary's team. Years later, that dream was realized as I played on the team that won the Scranton YMCA Brooke Memorial Tournament and the Scranton Rec- sponsored county-wide open tournament. In the latter, I led the team in scoring in the championship game.)

* * * * *

The parents were proud of their son's accomplishments and contributions to the parish reputation and growth. They and the entire family had a reverential pride in the middle of the pack daughter, Stasia, as she joined her maternal aunt, Sr. Wladzmiera, as a nun in the Felician Order in Lodi, New Jersey, and selected her religious name, Sr. Jolanta. (I accompanied Mom and Dad, and the rest of the family, as we attended and celebrated her ring ceremony. Years later, I felt honored as she told me that she loved my nickname "Breezy" and that it was soon after the ceremony that she named her guardian angel Breezy. He apparently did a good job, as she became the longest living family member and died at the age of 93.)

* * * * *

When John was in his early 20's and very active in parish activities, he participated in and attended fund raising social events sponsored by various societies. It was at one of them that he met and began socializing with a dark-haired, pretty lady of the same age named Mary Szczepanski.

* * * * *

Ignatz Szczepanski and Frances Jedrzejewski were born in the same rural community in the town of Wroclaw, near Warsaw, in a Russian-controlled section of Poland circa 1877. As youngsters, they received little, if any, formal education and, at an early age, began working on large, gentry-owned farms. As Ignatz grew into his teens, he was selected as a coachman and subsequently took the reins of the landowner's luxurious personal carriage.

When he and Frances began to socialize, he enjoyed singing and dancing to Polish music. His love of music led him to earnestly learn to play the violin. He and Frances entered into marriage circa 1896, and a year later were blessed with the birth of their first child, a daughter they named Stella, who died at birth. During the next four years, as Ignatz was driving the gentry coach and playing the violin at weddings and social events in their community, they were blessed with two sons, Stanley (1899) and John (1901).

Friends and relatives began migrating to the United States, and, a year or so later, the couple with their two toddler sons joined the migration. They were greeted by their earlier arriving relatives as they settled in the coal mining region of northeast Pennsylvania, in the valley town of Mocanaqua, where relatives, including Frances' brother, were settled, and where her younger sister and husband, along with their mother and younger brother, would also settle.

* * * * *

They joined St. Adelbert's Church in the nearby uphill town of Glen Lyon, as Ignatz went to work in the local coal mine and began playing his violin at area events. They moved into a duplex home in the "Patch," an area between both towns, in close proximity to the mine. It was there, in 1903, that they were blessed with their third son, Michael. On August 9, 1904, Frances also gave birth to Mary, their first surviving daughter.

The Patch was a series of seven coal company-built unpainted duplex houses in close proximity to each other and across the dirt road from the company mule barn.

There were no sidewalks, and any sustained or heavy rainfall left the area a sea of mud. The houses provided a barely adequate and basically confined shelter. They included a coal stove for heating and cooking but lacked any indoor amenities, including water, which they hoisted from a nearby well. It was the children's chore to carry home the families' daily water needs, and they would do so with pails hung on a shoulder yoke. The older ones, particularly the boys, would use a larger yoke and buckets.

By the end of 1911, the family had been in the area for almost ten years and continued living in the "Patch." Mary's mother had given birth to four more children, named Genevieve, Louis, Mabel, and Catherine, bringing the number of living children to eight. Her older brothers worked at the mine with her dad, and he also organized a small polka group that was becoming more popular and playing at events as far north as Dickson City, where some friends and relatives were relocating. Mary was 7 years old and walked down the mountain to attend the local school and was accompanied by friends, including Mary (Mae) Lojewski, whose family farm they traversed and whose family soon moved north to Dickson City.

One year later, in 1912, tragedy struck the family when their oldest son, Stanley, age 13, died from a broken neck he sustained three days earlier in a fall from a fruit tree. The family was devastated, and the parents would be haunted by this tragic and accidental loss for years to come.

By the end of 1915, Frances had given birth to two more sons, Ignatiues (Iggy) and Joseph, and she and her husband were still feeling remorse over their oldest son's death. Ignatz was playing at more weddings in Dickson City, and he recognized that there were more occupational and musical engagement opportunities in that more populated area. He and Frances decided that a change in location would be beneficial to the family, so the following year they and their nine children moved north to Dickson City.

* * * * *

They rented a duplex with indoor conveniences and joined St. Mary's Parish that was located at the other end of town. Ignatz and his three eldest sons obtained employment at or in local mines, and he began playing at more social events and giving private violin lessons. Mary, after recently finishing sixth grade, went to work at the Frisbee Silk Mill, became known as a "Frisbee Girl," and thereafter referred to the building as her alma mater. Soon she was joined by younger sisters as they came of age, and, with the various family members working and contributing to the coffers, the family's financial stability increased.

Two years later, in 1918, as Frances was preparing to give birth to their twelfth child, a daughter they named Frances, they bought and moved into the house across the street, at 642 Boulevard Avenue, where 2 years hence, she would give birth to their final child, a daughter they named Helen, and who would affectionately be called "Babe."

It was a well-built two-story home, little more than a decade old, with a basement, decent sized porch, and a driveway leading to a double garage with loft storage. It had a coal-fired central steam heat system; all indoor conveniences; and an additional cooking, eating, and food storage area in part of the basement. Their backyard was large enough for them to raise chickens and ducks and plant vegetable and flower beds, a grapevine, and a couple fruit trees.

The property line abutted a wooded portion of what would become the parish-owned Polonia Park, where food stands and a dance hall would be erected to host parish picnics and sponsored carnivals. The park abutted the Lacawanna River, a scenic stream that drained the valley of the same name. Unfortunately, over time, the water began to run black and kill aquatic life. The pollution increased over time as the river drained the acid-filled run-off water from coal company operations, and suffered further abuse by some residents and businesses. (Before the end of the century, after the imposition of clean water regulations and the construction of sewage treatment plants, the stream returned to its idyllic condition – to the extent that sections of it were designated as trophy trout areas.)

* * * * *

On weekends, when Ignatz did not have any musical engagements, he and Frances gathered the children to practice/participate in Polish dance lessons. He played the violin; she did the demonstrating and coaching, and they both did appropriate critiquing. The children were paired by age, beginning with John and Mary, and when the youngest were a few years old, they joined in. Heaven help anyone who was lackadaisical or fooling around, for he or she would soon feel the sting of the violin bow across their calves.

Mary would later recount that they weren't practicing jump rope or hopscotch, but were learning to properly dance with their feet. Learn they did, as they all developed into excellent dancers, the only discernible difference being their individual inherent rhythms. Their ability primarily lay in dancing the polka, oberek, and Slovak ciardash, and they easily adapted to the modern music of that era.

However, it was the abilities of the oldest and youngest parings that would garner the most attention and admiration. Johnny and Mary had a deep appreciation for music and loved to dance. They were light and quick with a relaxed, smooth rhythm. His was more pronounced and earned him the nickname "shimmy." Whenever they attended a wedding or dance, he would approach Mary and say, "Come on, Sis, let's show 'em how it's done." She would curtsy, and he'd take her by the hand. He had a comfortable and reassuring way of holding the woman in his arms, and after those many hours of practice, Mary would anticipate and smoothly respond to his moves. As dancers stepped back, observing and admiring their technique, he would say, "Here we go, Sis," and he would lead her through smooth spins (na lewo-na prawd) to the left or right. Later in life, as they neared their senior years, he'd offer her his hand and say, "Come on Sis, let's show these young kids that we still have it." Afterward, he'd walk her back to the table, kiss her cheek, and say, "We showed we still have it, Sis."

Joey and Fran, the youngest pairing, had that family rhythm and technique, and they loved to dance. Prior to their teenage years, they would take to the dance floor at weddings, oblivious to the attention they were garnering until people began throwing coins to them or pressing money into their hands. Initially, they were surprised that people gave them money for doing what they enjoyed, but they soon realized that they had a good thing going, and would dance all the more.

* * * * *

Throughout her teen years, Mary continued working at the mill, where she was joined by her younger sisters who also left school to join the family workforce. By the time she turned 20 in 1924, she was an excellent seamstress and took pride in her products. She knitted sweaters and cut and sewed patterned dresses, for herself and for other family members, and helped her siblings as they undertook their efforts. The friendship was re-kindled with former Glen Lyon friends Mae and her 9 year older sister, Bella Lojeski, the latter now, Mrs. Bill Buza. They would meet and socialize at Bella's new home as they marked and stitched quilts.

Mary was also very active in the church religious and social activities. She joined Bella as a member of the Dzieci Marji (Children of Mary) Society, wherein she was crowned the May Queen, served a one-year term as President, and participated in their various fund raising socials.

It was at one of these socials that she met a tall young man by the name of John Bartkowski. At that social, the raffle prize was a new, brand-name mattress. As she was circulating among the attendees, selling the raffle tickets, she approached John, and after mutual introductions naively asked, "Would you like to take a chance on a mattress?" She was momentarily embarrassed by his grin and raised eyebrows, as she realized the connotation in her question. She recovered quickly and while thrusting the raffle book at him said, "It's not what you're thinking; here, buy a ticket." He didn't win the mattress that night, but he soon won her heart as he walked her home from various socials and dances and basketball games, that she began attending.

* * * * *

On September 3, 1927, a Labor Day weekend, John and Mary, both age 23, were married in St. Mary's church by Monsignor Szpotanski.

One month after the wedding, tragedy again struck Mary's family. Her 20-year-old brother, Louie, an usher in their wedding party, died from burns received in a mine explosion a few days earlier. His dad, working in a nearby chamber, was slightly singed but was restrained from immediately responding to his son's screams for help by automatically closed containment doors.

Walter (Wacek) Chrzanowski from Pittsburgh, Pennsylvania, was visiting with the family at the time, as he was courting his soon-to-be-wife, Mary's sister, Genevieve, and he maintained a diary of the visit. (Thank you to cousins Sonia Kraemer and her brother Gene for sharing with us a copy of their dad's diary, as follows:)

"Thursday, Sept. 29, 1927

On return home, G.S. (Genevieve Szczepanski) was rubbing her eyes, remarking, 'Maybe I will cry, since I am rubbing my eyes so.' As we entered the house, we heard bad news. Louis S. (Szczepanski) was injured in a mine explosion along with seven others. His father was also in the same mine but on another branch, and the injuries received by him were a few burnt hairs above the left ear. L. S. was taken to the Mid Valley Hospital at Peckville along with six others injured. One of the men was found under a mine car the next morning, dead, his neck broken as well as other bones of his body.

A most pitiable sight was to behold anyone entering the Mid Valley Hospital. A man by the name of Jack Gawronski, who occupied the first bed nearest the door, was a scare. His face, neck, and hands were bandaged, but he did not show any signs of suffering. He stayed up in his bed and talked with others. He made a remark: 'If you fellows have a masquerade party, invite me, and I am sure I will win first prize,' which could not be doubted.

One of the injured men died at the hospital that night. This man, by the name of Jack Smith, had been continually asking for water, but the nurse just held him down with the bed covers, not giving him any water. Jack died that night at about 11:15. His condition, although not so bad looking on the outside, was the worst in his lungs. He had inhaled the poisonous mine gas. A couple of days later when visiting Jack as he was laid out, we were amazed to see the way the undertaker had fixed him up. We understood that the undertaker had taken three layers of skin off his face in order to make a clear complexion.

The official cause of the explosion was assigned to 'sparks flying out of the locomotive while skidding, igniting the gas in the mine and causing the explosion.' The explosion occurred about a mile from the surface. On account of the frequency of the gas in the mine, it is necessary to have safety lamps while working. Just shortly after the explosion, Jack Smith, the most seriously burned, had come to I.S. (Ignatz Szczepanski) asking for help. He was a human torch of flame. I.S. seeing his son the way he had been burned and upon seeing that he could go back to the opening by himself, had been tearing off the clothes off Jack Smith as rapidly as he could. One of the men laying track in the mine, working with a crow-bar, was thrown by the force of the explosion, and the bar lodged in his left leg.

Friday night (Sept. 30, 1927), in company with Jack Bart and Mickey, I spent in the hospital at the bedside of the patient. He was continually asking for liquids, if not for tea it was coffee, or milk, but doctor's orders were to give him water only.

Saturday morning (Oct. 1, 1927) we drove to the office of the mine where the accident had occurred, getting Louis's clothes which were always aired. I slept for about five hours Saturday.

Went to the hospital Saturday evening. After returning from the hospital I stayed up until about 2:00 A.M. Sunday (Oct. 2, 1927) morning I intended to go to church and leave Dickson City at about noon, but I received reports that Louis had died at the hospital. Did not attend church Sunday. Went to sleep early Sunday night.

Tuesday night (Oct. 4, 1927) stayed up during the night.

Wednesday morning (Oct. 5, 1927) had prepared to go to church for Mass at 8:30. Arrived at church at about 8:30, and it was almost the end of the Mass, the priest having Mass at 8:00 AM, not notifying the people. Returned home. It was a beautiful day for a funeral. About 2:00 PM, people were gathering to pay their last respects for the deceased. I was one of the flower carriers, it being the custom to have a fellow with two girls alongside of him carry a wreath of flowers that were given to the deceased. A band and procession of several hundred men preceded the gathering to church where the last rites were held for the deceased.

A sermon was also spoken. From church the gathering proceeded to the cemetery. Here among cries and sorrows, with the priest praying, the corpse was laid to final rest. There was but one automobile, carrying the priest and organist, all others walking to church and to the cemetery. A couple of motorcycle cops held order during the procession. After our return to the home of the deceased there were served eats for participants in the funeral."

* * * * *

The newlyweds moved into the upstairs apartment in John's parent's new home and continued being active in parish activities. John continued to work in the mine, played basketball on the parish team, and became very active in the community politics, where he was soon elected to the town council. Mary quit her job at the mill, concentrated on organizing housewife activities, and occasionally participated in quilting sessions at Bella's home. The following summer, at one of the sessions, Mary and Bella each proudly announced that they were with child, and were astonished as they realized that their delivery due dates were coincidentally in the latter half of December 1928. Over the next few months, they discussed and compared their pregnancy progression.

CHAPTER THREE

OUR BIRTHS

On the evening of Sunday, December 16, 1928, as John was playing in a basketball game at the parish hall, Dr. Gombar (the team physician) was summoned from the hall and, along with John's mother, assisted Mary in the delivery of their first child, a son. I would be named John, soon called Junior and subsequently, Breezy. Word was sent to the hall, and the game was temporarily halted, as my birth was announced to the fans' cheers and shouts of congratulations to Dad.

Eight days later, on the evening of December 24, 1928, as Bill Buza was tending to his tavern patrons, his wife, Bella, gave birth to their sixth child, a daughter they named Dorothy and subsequently called Dodo. As she emitted her first baby cry, the patrons in the family tavern responded with cheers and shouts of congratulations to her smiling dad. He distributed cigars, and the patrons toasted him with the round of drinks that were "on the house."

We were baptized in St. Mary's Church. My baptism was performed on December 30, 1928, and hers on January 13, 1929 (years later, in that church, we received our First Holy Communion on June 5, 1937, and June 12,

1938, respectively and the sacrament of confirmation on December 11, 1938, and on October 28, 1940.)

Dad's brother Chester (Uncle Chet) and Mom's sister Genevieve (Aunt Gen) were my godparents. Dodo's were family friends Anthony Zalewski and Mary Kucinska. In the Polish tradition, Chet thus became Gen's "Komoter," and she became his "Komoszka." These were honorary designations recognizing their special pairing and participation in a significant religious event. The same recognition existed between Dodo's godparents.

There were many joyous attendees at each of our baptisms and the celebrations that followed, but the most joyous emotion was reflected in the eyes of my maternal grandparents, because I was their first grandchild.

* * * * *

During the subsequent warm spring days, our moms occasionally strolled along together with us in our carriages. At times, they would peek into the other's carriage and express their oohs and aahs and exclaim, "What a beautiful baby you have!"

By various accounts, we were happy, well-fed, well cared for, content babies, and we soon began developing a strong bond with various family members. We would smile at the sight of them and react and respond to them with excited hand and leg movements. In some cases, the bonding was special and unique and was nurtured and grew stronger over time. This was the case between Dorothy and her nine year older brother, Ted, who, with his soft, shy smile and various facial expressions, would get her to smile and comply with his requests. With me, it was my godfather, Uncle Chet.

* * * * *

Dad, and particularly Mom, often retold the story of how they enjoyed observing Chet and I bond. Our bond formed soon after my birth. When they asked Chet to be my godfather, he was a 19-year-old hard nose and physically competitive lad, working alongside Dad in the mine. He camouflaged his compassionate and caring attributes. He showed emotion and pride as he thanked them for bestowing upon him that honor and for the faith they had in him, for by tradition, he would be responsible for my care in the event that something happened to them. His pride and emotion was detectable at my baptism as he carried me to the altar for the first time, gently yet securely cradled in his arms.

Chet had a strong desire and determination to become a smooth dancer to the various Polish rhythms, and he grasped at every opportunity to practice and learn. His favorite teacher was his Komoszka, Aunt Gen, and they practiced with other family members in the basement of her parents' home. At other times, I was his practice mate.

Frequently, when he heard me fussing or otherwise awake in my crib, he would come running up the steps to our apartment, lift and cradle me in his arms, and dance up and down the long hallway while he hummed various Polish tunes. At the end of a session, some of which lasted an hour, he or we would be sweating, and I would be asleep in his arms. Initially, he would perform some jerky movements that would startle me, and I would let out a cry. Soon, however, he became a smooth dancer. Over the next year or so, as he was improving, he'd hold me in his outstretched hands and exclaim, "na lewo" or "na prawo" ("to the left" or "to the right") and, with smooth dance steps, slew us in the appropriate direction, as I laughed and shrieked with joy.

* * * * *

After I began walking and talking, we moved a very short distance, up the block, into the family-owned "old home" duplex, at 1024 Carmalt Street. We resided there for roughly the next 10 years. Uncle Chet frequently visited with us and as we greeted each other with a warm hug, he'd ask, "How ya doin', Junior?" I would respond, "Fine, Uncle Chet." Later, as he was leaving, he'd remark, "Let me know if I can do anything for you, Junior," and I would respond, "Thank you, Uncle Chet." For years to come, those greeting and departing remarks became a ritual exchange in our interactions.

Between those remarks, we would discuss the activities in which I was involved. In elementary school, he inquired about my academic progress, congratulated me at my First Holy Communion and confirmation, and expressed his pride as I became the first altar boy in the family and joined the Boy Scouts.

Dad and I would visit Uncle Chet in the hospital during his slow recovery from back injuries incurred in the coal mine roof collapse. On a couple of these visits, in response to his pleadings, we brought along a couple of rings of his favorite "Ma's smoked kielbasa" (wrapped in butcher and newspaper), to supplement the "poor food" he was being served that was "hindering" his recovery. He ate a ring as we visited and stowed the other under his pillow for a late night snack. It must have been the correct remedy, for he was soon released, because the doctors were amazed at his sudden and speedy recovery.

When I was about nine years old, I accompanied Dad and a few uncles to the Town Hall in Scranton to attend Uncle Chet's boxing match, the one where he split his boxing trunks. I was disappointed that he lost and, afterwards in the locker room, as his bruises and swellings were being medically treated, I told him I was proud of his effort and thought he had been robbed.

As a youngster at his wedding, I congratulated him and his bride, Ann, wished them happiness, and danced with her in the bridal dance.

When I played basketball on the high school and college teams, he attended some games, and, afterwards, complimented me on my aggressive style of play. He congratulated me when I graduated from both schools, and when I was appointed team co-captain in my senior year of college.

* * * * *

On our wedding day, Uncle Chet congratulated us, told Dodo that she was a beautiful bride, and told me to take good care of her and treat her well. Soon thereafter, we moved out of the area, and he and I saw each other less often. I would visit him on occasion when he was temporarily hospitalized; we would exchange Christmas cards with penned notes, and Dad would call to tell me that Uncle Chet had asked how I was doing and if there was anything he could do for me.

We took the opportunity to continue our personal interaction at various family events, particularly at his generation's funerals and my generation's weddings including his daughter's. It was at these events that his renowned wit and humor were on display, as he would tell funny stories, some unbelievable, all involving him. As all were laughing, he would retain a deadpan expression.

* * * * *

I had been hearing that his health was failing, and when he was in his late seventies, and I in my late fifties, we attended the family's annual summer picnic. He arrived in a wheelchair, a blanket loosely draped over his lap and obviously in the last stages of life.

As we hugged, he asked, "How ya doin', Junior?" "Fine" I replied, "but this time it's my turn; how are you doing, Uncle Chet? Is there anything I can do for you?" "As a matter of fact, there is, Junior," he replied. "I was hoping you'd be here today, as I have a special favor to ask of you."

He went on to recall the honor that he felt was bestowed upon him when he was asked to be my godfather and again at my baptism, when he carried me to the altar for the first time. "I'd appreciate it if you would honor me one more time, Junior. I'd like you to be a pallbearer and carry me to the altar for the last time." I hugged him and, with emotions straining, replied, "It would be my honor, Uncle Chet." He clasped my hand, and, with a smile, said, "Thank you, Junior."

A few months later, I felt truly honored as we approached the altar with his casket.

CHAPTER FOUR

THE GREAT
DEPRESSION DECADE

In late October 1929, as the decade of the roaring 20's was coming to a close and our families were anticipating celebrating our 1st birthdays, the country's economy was dealt a severe blow as the stock market collapsed. The value of the individual's and financial institutions' investments plummeted and, in some cases, those investments were completely wiped out. People who had deposited their savings in local banks, or invested them in stocks were similarly affected.

The ripple effect soon spread throughout the country and the world, for with the loss of wealth, there was a sharp decline in the demand for goods and services. Solvent companies continued operating with occasional slowdowns, while less solvent ones were forced to close. Layoffs began, adding to the problem, and the unemployment rate rapidly increased to near 20%, where it hovered for the rest of the decade of the 30's. This time period would become historically known as the Great Depression. As the unemployment rate rose, and there weren't any unemployment benefits, so did home and farm foreclosures.

In the large cities, thousands stood in lines to apply for several newly-posted job opportunities. Hundreds more stood in bread, soup, and shelter lines; others stood on street corners selling pencils and apples; while others, including youngsters, stood on sidewalks, holding homemade shoe shine boxes and offering to give shines for pennies.

In the small towns, such as ours, residents increasingly grew vegetable gardens and a fruit tree or two, raised chickens and ducks, and used the duck feathers to fill homemade pillows and comforters. Occasionally, people would exchange waves with men, (some called them hoboes), who had hopped onto and were riding freight trains from city to city in search of employment. The men would disembark in various towns, rest at nearby hobo camps, and seek food from locals in exchange for chores. Some men weren't conscientious and residents occasionally reported a chicken or two stolen or a garden raided.

In the rural areas, the farmers were growing crops and raising livestock, but the cash crop market significantly diminished, and many struggled to stay afloat, while some even experienced foreclosure.

Over time, the federal government initiated several programs in an effort to halt the economic downward spiral. Surplus farm crops, canned juices, vegetables, and fruits were bought by the government and locally distributed to needy families. Make work programs were initiated. Two notable ones were the WPA (Work Project Administration) and the CCC (Civil Conservation Corps.). In the former, mostly married, unemployed breadwinners were hired to repair country roads and bridges and to dig associated drainage ditches. The young, single men joined the CCC and were billeted in military-style encampments that they constructed in various woodlands. These young men were issued military-type clothes, furnished with meals and sleeping quarters, and were required to send most of their wages to their families. Conservation being the primary goal, the men cleared dead wood, planted seedlings, developed parks and camping facilities, cleared hiking trails, and built bridges spanning various streams.

* * * * *

Our town and the surrounding communities' residents were exposed to and affected by the events emanating from the financial downturn. Family-owned small businesses, along with the light industries and major coal companies, remained operational. The latter two did experience decreased product demand that resulted in occasional slowdowns or outright layoffs.

Several events occurred that determined a family's economic position. Families lost all or most of their wealth as some of the banks holding their savings accounts began failing. The townspeople, as did the nation, began a run on the banks to withdraw their money, and these runs contributed to the "panic" in '33 that resulted in the government declaring a bank holiday and closing the banks for a period of time in order to stop the runs. Families, also fearing the loss of the breadwinner's job, decreased their purchases and standard of living. Some families experienced total despair when the father was disabled or killed in a coal mine accident, suddenly leaving the family without a breadwinner.

The fear was spreading, and, in March of '33, the newly elected President, Franklin D. Roosevelt, in an attempt to bolster confidence, asserted in his inaugural address to the nation that "we have nothing to fear but fear itself."

* * * * *

At times, when Dad was at work in the mine, the company whistle would begin blaring a signal denoting a serious accident and the need for emergency response. Mom would tear up and pray for the safety of Dad and the other men. When such an event occurred while I was in parochial school, our class activity would cease as we prayed for the safety of the men. Those of us whose fathers were at work in the mine would feel a chill and pangs of fear. Later, as the names of the injured or dead became known, our class would pray for them and for the families, aware of the suffering and hardship they were and would be enduring.

In one mine accident, Dad and his three crew members narrowly escaped being killed as a slab of roof fell into the chamber in which they were working. However, his brother, Chet, spent more than a week in the hospital recovering from mostly back and shoulder injuries he had received while wedged under a portion of the slab that came to rest on a boulder. As one of the crew went seeking help, Dad, using his size and strength, braced against the chamber roof, and, using a prop timber as a lever, raised the slab enough to allow a crew member to pull Chet to safety.

* * * * *

There weren't any unemployment, disability, or insurance checks to assist the needy families. Along with help from extended family members, various levels of government, community business, and civic and religious organizations, needy family members, including small children, pooled their efforts and did what they had to do to help the family survive the economic hardship.

A couple of times each month, family members, pulling reinforced battered wagons, would join a line at the municipal building to obtain government-distributed surplus food products that included bags of flour, sugar and salt, and canned meats, vegetables, fruits and juices. Some cans were missing labels.

To provide for the coal needs for cooking and heating, teenage family members would scour freshly-dumped coal mine slag and would scan railroad beds for chunks of coal that had fallen from passing coal trains.

During the summer months, teenagers living in close proximity to the shallow running river would wade across, carrying their younger siblings. On the opposite, hilly bank they would pick pieces of coal from the freshly-dumped slag, and, at the end of the day's efforts, they would wade back across the river carrying their siblings and burlap bags full of coal. For the next few days, the youngsters, using hammers, would crack the coal into usable sizes, store it in the shed, and repeat the effort. One summer, as a youngster, I spent a couple of days helping Mom's youngest brother, Uncle Joey, crack and store the coal that he had picked and carried across the river.

* * * * *

Periodically, a man would walk along the alley and announce his presence by clanging a hand held bell. Strapped to his shoulders, he would carry a fixture which included a pop-up seat and a pedal-operated honing wheel that allowed him to sharpen knives and scissors. Similarly, an older gentleman would ride atop an old farm wagon, pulled along by a plodding, tired-looking old horse. His presence was announced by the jingling of the harness bells and the clanging of the metal wares in the wagon. He bought rags, pots, and pans, and other metallic items and sold them along his route or to the junkyard owner, whose site was located in the boulevard section of the town.

* * * * *

Many of the numerous grocery store owners, tavern owners, and other small business owners would extend zero interest credit to their regular and reliable customers by allowing their purchases to be recorded on the book. The book was usually retained by the customers, though some owners retained carbon copy pages. The total bill was usually paid in full on the customer's next pay day. The destitute families made periodic partial payments with the expressed intent to pay the entire bill as their economic situation improved.

* * * * *

On the other hand, people, including coal miners, who had steady and decently-paying jobs, would feed and clothe their families well, and would buy cars and/or homes. They would spend a week-long summer vacation at a local lake or some other destination, and would take pleasure drives on Sunday.

Some professionals and prosperous business owners bought or built summer cottages at local lakes and joined their families there on hot weekends and sultry weeknights in order to escape the valley's summer heat spells.

* * * * *

As youngsters, Dodo and I were shielded from the devastating effects of the Depression. Ours were fortunate families, because our fathers were steadily employed throughout the decade. It wasn't until we began attending elementary school, during the worst part of the Depression, that we began to realize the hardships being experienced by some of our fellow students and their families. At our young age, however, we accepted it as a normal way of life.

The oldest family sibling in school wore store-bought clothes supplemented by homemade garments. The younger siblings wore well-maintained hand-me-downs. The boys' homemade garments usually were knitted sweaters, and Mom knitted warm, beautiful ones over the years. The girls' garments were skirts and tops, along with undergarments made from Pillsbury or Gold Medal flour sacks.

We had a pair of shoes for Sunday wear and another for school. When they wore out, we would have them re-soled and heeled at the shoe repair shop. For play, we would wear sneakers and, when they frayed, we would patch or wrap them with electrical tape until they literally fell apart.

All of our new garments and shoes were a size or two larger than needed. They were bought to accommodate our growth spurts, per the Polish saying, "na wyrost," meaning, "for growing into." We would stuff our new shoes with paper or cotton and adjust as necessary. Our pants were a prime example of our three stages of debonair clothing: Folded cuffs, just right, or high waters.

* * * * *

Dodo's father, Bill, maintained a prosperous, family-oriented tavern, and he tended to the desires and needs of his mostly-employed customer base. He served daily lunch and, on Saturday evenings, he would serve food that featured his wife, Bella's famous homemade bread, hearty soups, select meals, and, occasionally, steamed clams.

Dad, President of the town council, worked steadily as a coal miner, except during the long strike in the early '30s when the miners sought a reduction in the work week from 6 to 5 days and safer work conditions. It was during this strike that we temporarily felt the pangs and anxiety of the unemployed.

Dad quite often came home from work to find a father, or a widow and her son, greeting him on the porch, where they had waited for his arrival for several hours, and in despair, asked for his help in acquiring a job. Dad and Dodo's father (retired from political office), both used their political influence and connections to successfully sponsor a number of people for job openings in the coal mines; federal, state, and county level services and the WPA. At other times, Dad would have a ton of coal delivered to a needy family or invite them to take enough potatoes, adequate for a family meal, from a sack he kept on the side porch.

* * * * *

Thanks to the personal drive and continuous hard work of our fathers, and the similar display of supportive and dedicated efforts of our mothers, both of us lived a middle-class, some even called it a prosperous, lifestyle during the Depression. We wore quality dress clothes, some handmade by our mothers, and we were well-groomed and fed. Our mothers prepared chicken or a roast or some other special meal and dessert on Sunday, a turkey with all the trimmings on Thanksgiving, and a smoked ham on Christmas and Easter.

At Christmas, both families had decorated trees with presents underneath. Dodo's family traditionally decorated these trees with all silver icicles and blue lights, while ours had multi-colored lights and ornaments, with a manger and a miniature village and an electric train underneath. At Easter, there was a new outfit and a candy basket, filled with multi-colored jelly beans and featuring a solid chocolate egg or rabbit.

* * * * *

There were some notable differences in our families' lifestyles. Dodo's family lived in their modern, solidly-constructed and well-furnished multi-room home with all indoor amenities, including central heat. We rented our two bedroom, barely insulated duplex, with its cold running water, coal stove heat, and a duplex outhouse.

Dodo's father had an aversion to driving a car and never owned one. In reality, he didn't need one, since they lived in the center of the town's business and civic activities. Public transportation was available at the corner of their block, and their relatives lived within a short walk. When on occasion they needed private transportation, it was provided by a customer, friend, relative, or by his oldest son, Vince, when he became of age and drove his own car.

On the other hand, part way through the Depression, Dad bought his first car, albeit a used one, from Mom's brother Johnny, and soon loved to drive. During the week, he would drive to work, political activities, and occasionally a local lake for some evening fishing. At other times, he would take us on Sunday rides and vacations.

* * * * *

There were other memorable events that occurred in the '30s. Dodo celebrated the birth of her baby sister Evelyn (Oct 1931), the marriage of Vince, her oldest sibling, and her oldest sister, Toni's, graduation from college. I celebrated the births of sisters Elaine and Lorraine and brother Gene. Unfortunately, we also mourned the death of dearly loved ones.

* * * * *

In April 1934, when I was in first grade, my four-month-old baby sister, Elaine, died of pneumonia, developed during a short illness. Mom and Dad were extremely upset as they buried her, clad in my and her baptismal gown. Over the ensuing years, Mom would become teary-eyed when, on occasion, we would discuss that event. Dad would recall the added despair and anger he felt at the time, as the bank, in which they had deposited his hard-earned savings, was in the bank holiday lockdown mode, and he had to borrow money from relatives in order to pay the burial expenses.

* * * * *

On October 30, 1936, several weeks prior to my 8th birthday, and shortly after I served at my first Mass as an altar boy, Mom's mother unexpectedly died at the age of 59 after a short illness. As her first grandchild, I had developed a warm and loving relationship with her that, by various accounts, had begun during my infancy, as Grandma held me on her lap and rocked us on the rocking chair and conversed with Mom during our frequent visits. As I grew into the toddler stage, I seemingly anticipated and enjoyed our rocking as I cuddled on her lap and played with her fingers. When I began to talk, Mom and Dad taught me to also speak Polish, and I would converse with Grandma in her native language. After I started attending school, she was always very interested and would ask me about my progress.

On a couple of occasions, Grandma and I shared her homemade soda and sandwiches as we, and a couple of her children, took a lunch break during a day of picking huckleberries on a local mountainside. Serving as an altar boy at my first funeral Mass, I felt a deep loss when the priest and I stood at her casket while he recited the final prayers.

* * * * *

On April the 26th, 1938, when Dodo was 9 years old, in 4th grade and preparing to receive her First Holy Communion within a few weeks, her mother, Bella, died. She had entered the hospital for a mastoid operation, and, while there, contracted spinal meningitis, a deadly infection that resulted in her death at the age of 43. Her family, friends, and acquaintances were shocked, for she was an active woman in good health.

Mom was really upset at the news of Bella's death, for she often visited with Bella and knew all of her children. She told Dad and me that she felt sorry for all of the family, but even more so for the two youngest, a daughter named Dorothy, nicknamed "Dodo," whom Bella had delivered a week after Mom had delivered me, and a younger daughter named Evelyn.

As an altar boy at the time, I was selected to serve at that funeral. I carried the cross, and, at the church, I led Bella's casket down the aisle to the base of the altar. After the Mass was completed, the prayer ritual was held alongside the casket, and I held the cross at my position at one end of the casket. I glanced over to catch a glimpse of this young girl, Dodo, that my Mom had talked about, and I saw her sitting amongst her siblings in a state of grief. I was feeling sorrow for her and experiencing my own grief as I realized that it could be my Mom's casket that I was standing next to.

The ceremony concluded, and I turned and led Bella's casket up the aisle, past grieving mourners, to the waiting hearse. Who, in that crowded church, in their wildest imagination, could have envisioned that one day in the future, I would happily lead her daughter up that same aisle, arm in arm, acknowledging our smiling and happy families and friends, after being pronounced husband and wife?

* * * * *

In February of 1938, we experienced a scare that, fortunately, did not result in a death. My 2 ½ year old sister, Lorraine, was rushed to the hospital and her appendix removed.

That night, Mom knelt with me as we said my bedtime prayers, and offered a special one for Lorraine's recovery. Mom embraced and consoled me as I cried and expressed my fear that another sister of mine was about to die.

A week or so later, Lorraine was brought home and was on the road to recovery.

CHAPTER FIVE

FAMILY GATHERINGS

In spite of the hard times of the 30s, family traditions and celebrations continued unabated to celebrate baptisms, First Communions, confirmations, and graduations. There were other special recurring events that deserve noting.

* * * * *

On Christmas Eve, my paternal grandparents would host the family Wygilja, a seven-dish traditional Polish meal that consisted of fried bony fish and six other tasteless dishes. As the first visible star rose in the eastern sky, their fourteen children, along with a half dozen or more of their spouses and close to a dozen grandchildren, would gather to partake. Prior to the serving of the meal, we would each receive an oplatek, (a blessed wafer), and share pieces of it with each other as we wished for health and happiness in the new year and apologized for any family transgressions we may have committed during the past year.

At meal time, we would all sit in one large room at a series of unadorned wooden banquet tables. There was always an extra chair and place setting at the head of the main adult table to accommodate any needy stranger or family acquaintance who may come to the door. Occasionally someone did, and one year it happened to be a reporter who was preparing a story on the event for a local newspaper. At the grandchildren's table, our plates sat on a bed of straw and, as we finished eating, we would raise our plates to find in the straw, a small denomination coin and penny candy.

Later in the evening, we would visit my maternal grandparents, share an oplatek and refreshments, and exchange Christmas greetings with them, their unmarried children, and the married ones who were also visiting. On Christmas Eve in 1936, two months after Grandma died unexpectedly, we had a tearful and mournful visit with Grandpa. He was depressed, with a broken spirit, and his condition continued until he died in October 1941, within days of the 5th anniversary of Grandma's death.

* * * * *

Soon after Grandma's death, we moved into Mom's family home. She was anxious to rekindle her family holiday gatherings and hosted a Christmas Eve party for her siblings and their children. Everyone would arrive by 9 p.m. after fulfilling other earlier commitments. We would share the blessed wafers and appropriate Christmas wishes and indulge in the homemade snacks and liquid refreshments.

The women would chat as they sipped their wine or mixed drinks, changed diapers, or nursed babies. On the other hand, the men would drink freely and soon got into the hard stuff. As their consumption increased they would seriously debate innocuous, sometimes silly, topics. Soon, some of them would be on the living room floor challenging one another's skills in controlling the movement of an electric train that ran on a single track under the decorated tree.

As we joined in singing carols, we were accompanied by Mom's brother-in-law, Saik, on violin and her brother Johnny on piano and/or mouthorgan. Johnny was an excellent, naturally-talented musician who played by ear. In spite of losing the fingertips on his left hand, he retained his ability to play various instruments and occasionally would display the extent of his talent by playing select songs entirely on the black keys on the piano.

At the stroke of midnight, the fasting would end, and the Christmas celebration would begin. The buffet table was set with plates of baked ham and kielbasa, bowls of homemade potato and macaroni salads, and various homemade desserts. The party would end by 2 a.m., with several husbands being led home by their wives. Thereafter, hosting this family event was rotated among the siblings.

* * * * *

During the Easter holiday weekend, my family would engage in several traditions. On Good Friday, we would color eggs by wrapping each in several layers of brown onion skins and enclosing them in a layer of cheesecloth prior to boiling. After the eggs cooled, we would unwrap them and, on each, there would be an irregular pattern of variegated shades of earth colors.

On Holy Saturday, we would place an egg for each family member, along with some butter, homemade sweet bread, ham, kielbasa, and horse radish in a classic, handwoven basket that was lined and then covered with Mom's finest linens. Prior to a scheduled hour, we and scores of other parishioners would arrive at the school facility with the food baskets. Soon, the food would be exposed; our Priest would arrive and bless the food, and the facility would be permeated with the heavenly aroma of kielbasa.

We would consume the blessed food at our Easter meal that began with an egg cracking contest. Each of us would select an egg and, using the tip, tap the barely exposed tip of a family member's egg. Eventually, the person holding the only uncracked egg would proclaim victory and enjoy bragging rights. Mom would later gather the shells and other blessed food scraps and bury them in our garden rather than throw them out with the garbage.

On Easter Monday, we would celebrate "Dingus Day," a national holiday in Poland, where it was first celebrated in the 1800s and is still celebrated in Polish communities throughout the world. One of the largest takes place in Buffalo, New York. Men would "dingus" the women by spraying or sprinkling them with water. Some young single men would use cologne to impress maidens. Young boys would chase and swat the calves of young girls with a pussy willow branch. The women would retaliate in kind late that day or the next.

Polish folklore has it that this activity is a form of spiritual cleansing, akin to baptism, and commemorates the baptism of a young Polish prince on an Easter Monday in the 10th century. The entire royal family was baptized shortly thereafter. Their baptism led to the conversion of Poles to Catholicism.

* * * * *

The most lavish events were the wedding celebrations that were often held on and encompassed the entire Labor Day weekend.

Early in the year, with the blessings of their parents, the prospective bridal couple would announce their marriage intentions and begin planning the festivities. The couple would visit and personally invite their married siblings, uncles and aunts, cousins, neighbors, and friends, including all of their children, while relatives who lived further away would receive handwritten invitations. Bridal party members would be selected, as would be the patterns for the gowns and dresses to be handmade. The bride's family, responsible for hosting the festivities and supplying the food, would buy peeps and ducklings to be fattened for the event, and would expand their garden to grow more vegetables, including cabbage.

The preparation activities would peak during the week preceding the wedding. The groom's family would deliver the beer, liquor (some homemade), soda, and storage ice to the site, and the musicians they hired for the three-day event would be practicing and tuning their instruments. Furniture would be removed from the first floor of the bride's home to accommodate an indoor dining and dancing area, and additional rented banquet tables and chairs would be arranged in the backyard, usually under a tent. A wooden dance platform and temporary beverage bar would be constructed, the latter usually in the garage, and overhead lights would be strung. On the wedding day, family members and neighbors would complete the food preparations, and some of it would only need to be re-heated during the festivities.

After the church ceremony, the guests would begin arriving at the bride's home. Their arrivals would be noted by the musicians as they played a Polish wedding welcome song, thus alerting the family to the arrival of new guests. Soon, the food would be served family style by hired local women who performed the various kitchen activities as a couple of their husbands dispersed the beverages.

The food was usually a variety of soups, salads, and meats, and some, especially those that were fried in lard, were a cholesterol bomb, a concern unknown or ignored at the time. There was usually chicken and duck (czarnina) soups, potato, macaroni, and coleslaw salads; ham, smoked, and fresh kielbasa, golombki (pigs in the blanket), klopsi (meatballs) and fried chicken. Dancing and drinking would be ongoing, and soon some of the guests would simultaneously be doing both.

The evening activities would begin winding down following two traditional events. In one moving event, the bride would sit in the middle of the dance area as her mother removed her headpiece and veil and replaced it with a bonnet, while a select group of women would gather behind them, singing a Polish song that, in essence, acknowledged the bride's transition from a maiden to a woman.

The other event was referred to as the "bridal dance." Men and women would form a line to dance with the bride to a few bars of a traditional Polish song and, in the process, deposit a monetary donation into the bride's handmade "booty bag" held by the maid of honor. As a final group of young men finished the dance with the bride, they would form a tight circle that would escort the last man in the line as he "stole" and carried away the shrieking bride and her "booty." The groom was required to pay a nominal ransom fee, the value determined by the guests, before he could rescue and reclaim his bride, while cheered on by the assembled guests.

On the second day (poprawiny), a mock wedding would be re-enacted, and the partying and dancing would resume in a more relaxed and casual manner. On the third and final day, as the food and beverage supplies were dwindling, the out-of-towners would depart for home,; the newlyweds would depart on their honeymoon, and the cleanup and property restoration would begin.

* * * * *

At two of my generation's wedding receptions, spontaneous, humorous events occurred. At one, the inebriated father of the bride announced that he would perform a bridal dance. He rolled up his trouser legs, donned a bonnet and a large apron to hold the donations, and invited the women to dance with him. They sure did, many more than once, and, as the dance was nearing an end, his apron was overflowing with bottle caps and cigar and cigarette butts. His wife announced that if anyone stole him, they would have to keep him, since she would not pay a ransom for his release. Since there were no takers, she retrieved and carried her smiling and spent husband back to their table.

The other event occurred at a younger cousin's reception in an upper-class hotel ballroom in downtown Scranton. We were asked by our uncle not to steal the bride, for she would be very upset as she opposed the tradition, and we assured him, and our parents, that we would not. Apparently, our assurances did not convince the out-of-town groom's ROTC college friends, for as the bridal dance began, the cadets, in their military uniforms, and putting their training to use, established a perimeter around the dance area and posted sentries at each exit door.

With some of us having prior military experience, we thought it was time to have a little fun with the young cadets. When our last group of usual suspects neared the bride, the cadets devoted attention to the last one of us in line, but we soon had them confused as we continually changed positions. As we finished our dance turn, we formed an inner perimeter which brought the troops to full alert, as they compressed theirs. The dance ended with no attempt to steal the bride, and the cadets recalled the sentries and were gleefully congratulating each other on the success of their mission.

When the groom failed to respond to repeated calls for him to come forth to dance with the bride, the word spread that he was nowhere to be found and that apparently somebody had stolen the groom. Almost immediately there was bedlam in the ballroom.

The cadets, now in shock, initiated a rescue mission as some scurried in and out of restrooms and hotel rooms in search of the groom while others questioned guests as to when and where he had last been seen. Our jolly and stout aunt was restraining a cadet on her lap, in a firm embrace, as she asked his name and details about his childhood.

We, the usual suspects, were quickly exonerated since we had been observed participating in the bridal dance; but we were in hilarious disbelief at the activities and exchanges taking place. However, the bride and her dad, who moments earlier had acknowledged and smiled at us, were upset and giving us obviously unhappy glances. Mom and Dad, aware of our assurance that we wouldn't steal the bride, were struggling to contain their shocked and hilarious reaction.

The groom's mother, surrounded by her relatives, was exhorting them to call the police. Uncle Chet, our beloved off-duty city policeman, whose major duties were as a center city parking meter-maid and an intersection traffic and pedestrian control officer, approached her and said, "No need to, ma'am, I am the police," and asked, "What seems to be the problem?" Those of us within earshot, aware of his wit and dry humor, quickly realized that their exchange was going to be fun to hear, and we were not disappointed.

She told him that she wanted the police to immediately locate and rescue her kidnapped son as she was concerned about his safety, for in such trying circumstances, he was prone to display temper tantrums. With a serous expression, Uncle Chet told her not to worry, as his brethren were well trained to apply sharp nightstick taps to the forehead that quickly quelled such behavior; to which she responded with a gasp. He further told her that in order to trigger an immediate police search, he would file a missing person report (gasp) and needed a full description of the victim (gasp), including birthmarks and his full name.

Poised with a moistened pencil and a notepad in hand, he seemingly began taking notes. As the mother stated her son's full name, Uncle Chet briefly paused and then asked, "How does Tommy spell his first name?" When she began spelling it, he asked, "Are all of the letters in caps or just the first one?" all the while maintaining a serious composure, while we who were within earshot were struggling to contain ours. Similar exchanges followed, and several times she assured him that her son was in fact a male Caucasian. Finally he assured her that her son would be found and returned safely, and nodding his head for emphasis and with a firmer voice, added, "and the alleged perpetrators will be apprehended and appropriately dealt with," at which point we had to turn away because we had completely lost our composure, even though he maintained his.

Soon, the smiling groom re-entered the ballroom, aided by two of our cousins, one of them by marriage. The bride and mother rushed to embrace the groom and were chastising our cousins for kidnapping him. Our cousins denied any intended malice, rather, as a gesture of welcoming the groom into the family, they invited and he accompanied them to a tavern to partake in adult beverages, and in the process lost track of the time and were unaware that the bridal dance had ended. The groom nodded agreement, and Uncle Chet was overheard saying that the groom was found and returned safely as he had predicted.

Following the reception, we, along with our spouses, were invited and joined the cadets and their female companions in their hospitality suite. While socializing and partaking in adult beverages with them, I happened to retrieve and display a cousin's police badge that had somehow fallen out of his pocket, and requested I.D. proof that they were of the legal minimum drinking age of 21. As bottles were being hidden and drinks poured down the sink, I immediately revoked the request, as a hospitable gesture, that brought from them smiles and a huge sigh of relief. As we were departing, the cadet leader, while smiling and bobbing his head, said, "You guys are really good." We wished them luck and thanked them for volunteering to protect our country and, after a pause, someone added, "Let's hope you do a better job than you did protecting the groom."

Eventually, the bride and her dad resumed conversing with us, and we made sure that we didn't discuss this event in their presence.

CHAPTER SIX

THE DUPLEX

In early 1931, a few months after celebrating my 2nd birthday the previous December, we vacated the apartment in my paternal grandparents' "new house." We moved a short distance up the street, to the top of the hill, and rented half of the family's "old house" duplex at 1024 Carmalt Street. It was where Dad was born and raised, and it would be our residence for the next ten years.

We had front and side entrances that we accessed via a semi-wraparound porch. The latter also served as a play area where I rode on my tricycle.

Within our residence, there were two upstairs bedrooms, and on the main level, we had a parlor, kitchen (with a coal-fired stove), and a pantry where the wooden ice box and the sink with its cold water tap were located, along with shelves where Mom stored food, household items, and her preserves.

* * * * *

The stove was our major appliance. n fact, excluding the wooden ice box, it was our only appliance. It provided the heat to warm our residence, boil our hot water, and allow Mom to do the food preparations.

Dad usually built a new fire in the stove, but Mom was capable of doing it, if needed. Over time, they taught me to do it as I helped them.

Dad would build the fire by first closing the upper air flow vents while fully opening the bottom vents that were located on the side of the stove, adjacent to the fire box. These vent settings were most effective in building a new fire because they allowed maximum air flow to the box. Conversely, the vents would be set to the opposite extremes to smother the fire.

Dad would then ignite the layers of crumbled newspapers, kindling, and larger pieces of wood that he had placed on the pair of rotating grates. When the wood was fully ablaze, he would begin adding layers of coal. With a bed of burning coal established, and providing the minimal desired heat output, he would readjust the air flow vents to their middle range and add more coal. The moderate fire that resulted would burn for hours.

Once a fire was established, it could be kept burning indefinitely – for weeks on end. Several times a day, we would add coal, shake down the ashes that had accumulated on the grates that hadn't dropped into the container below, and adjust the air flow vents to increase the heat output that Mom needed for her cooking and baking. At night, the air vents were adjusted to dampen the fire and would be readjusted in the morning to rejuvenate it.

My daily chores included keeping the coal bucket full and the ash container empty. In keeping with the prevailing attitude – that nothing was to be wasted – we would use the ashes to fill depressions in the alley, and add them to our flower and vegetable garden soil. During the winter, when it was snowy or icy, we would spread them on the steps, sidewalk, and downhill back yard path as anti-slip material.

During the cold and occasionally frigid winter temperatures, the coal fire heat was adequate to keep our kitchen comfy warm, and even more so when Mom was doing her cooking. That wasn't the case in the rest of the rooms. The heat would drift into the parlor and the pantry through the open doorways, and up to the bedrooms through the stairway and the kitchen ceiling register.

At bedtime, the bedroom temperature would be relatively warm. After Dad dampened the kitchen coal fire for the night, however, the temp would begin to drop and, by the early morning hours, the air would be very cool, bordering on cold. I was warm throughout the night, however, because I slept under Mom's handmade *pierzina* – a lightweight, fluffy, thick comforter, filled with white duck down feathers. My pillow was filled with these feathers as well.

I hated crawling out of the warm bed, especially on the really cold mornings. Before hastening downstairs to dress next to the warm stove, I would stop at a bedroom window and, using a finger nail, I would etch my name and animal figures into the layer of frost that had accumulated on the inside window pane.

Eventually, Dad had a coal fired heater stove installed in their bedroom, and it provided wonderful warmth to both bedrooms, especially at bedtime. Before going to bed, Dad would also dampen that fire for the night. The temperatures would drop during the night, and, on very cold mornings, were low enough for me to do my etchings.

* * * * *

The heated surfaces on the kitchen stove made up Mom's work area, where she would place the cookware on the area that had the desired heat intensity. She simmered stews and varieties of soups, and boiled the vegetables and potatoes. The meats (some breaded) were fried in a heavy black iron skillet, in fresh or, more likely, saved and re-used lard or Crisco.

Other meats were prepared in the oven, where Mom would also bake bread, cakes, cobblers, and pies. Mom would bake bread and pies in quantities sufficient to last for a few days. On special occasions, she would bake sweet, rolled bread loaves with a ground poppy seed and honey mixture, or finely chopped walnuts. She would deep fry dozens of punchki (prune-filled, ball-shaped doughnuts) or krushchiki (bow-tie-shaped dough) that she would sprinkle with powdered sugar.

When using the oven, Mom would monitor the oven door temperature gauge. She would adjust and readjust the air flow vents to attain and maintain the desired oven temperature. At times, she would open the oven door to release excess heat or to test the texture of the baking items with a broom straw.

* * * * *

During the Depression we ate well and never went to bed hungry. Mom prepared and served tasty and wholesome meals that, at times, included her potato, macaroni, or coleslaw salads (the latter embedded with plenty of pineapple bits) and creamed, thinly sliced cucumbers.

The stews were thick and hearty. Mom's specialty soup was czarinina the chocolate-colored duck soup, whose base included the duck's blood that Dad drained from it, drop by oozing drop. We craved that special soup treat, and Mom would occasionally share it with family members, especially her brother, Uncle Iggy, and Dad's brother, Uncle Chet, both of whom also craved it. The latter craved for and consumed everything that anybody prepared for him, and tales of his appetite were legendary.

Our meats were prepared well done, yet quite juicy. Rare or even slightly rare was a no-no, because Mom feared that it would make us sick. For dessert, Mom would prepare and serve either Jello, (with embedded sliced bananas), pudding, cobblers, cake, or pies.

Our daily meal menu varied. For breakfast, we would eat either cold cereal with milk and bananas, hot oats, or farina (the latter was Dad's favorite ,and Mom claimed that it stuck to our ribs. I know that it stuck to the pot if we didn't stand at the stove and constantly stir it.)

At other times, we would have bacon, eggs (from our hens), and toast. We would toast the bread by placing and securing several slices in a toaster rack and holding the rack over the open fire in the stove – being careful not to burn the underside before flipping the rack. We would spread sweet tub butter and/or Mom's jam preserves on the toast.

For lunch, that we called dinner, we would have leftover stew or soup, most likely cold cut sandwiches, usually on Mom's baked bread.

At our evening meal that we called supper, we would occasionally have thick stew, hearty soup, or, most often, it was meat, mashed potatoes with gravy, and a vegetable, all followed by dessert. The meat would vary and included pork chops or butts, chicken, fresh or smoked kielbasa, veal, klopsi (meatballs), golomki (pigs in the blanket), ham, pigs feet, etc.

On Fridays and other meat fasting days, Mom would serve fried fish (some caught by Dad), bony herring (sledgie), stacks of potato pancakes (placki), farmer's cheese or potato-filled pierogis, or a heaping serving of mashed potatoes that we would dip by the spoonful in buttermilk.

* * * * *

During the growing season, we would handpick fruits (huckleberries, peaches, cherries, and apples) that Mom used in pies and cobblers and we would buy fresh vegetables for our daily use. Dad would handpick edible wild mushrooms and buy fruit and vegetables in bulk, and Mom would can them as jams or preserves in mason jars. Occasionally, we would substitute the commercially canned products that we bought at Grandma's grocery store.

Over the winter months, Mom's stores of preserved vegetables would dwindle, and we would buy more and more of the commercial varieties. At times, Dad would purchase a case of a canned vegetables at or below wholesale price because most, if not all, of the cans were missing their labels. Quite often thereafter, the product would be a frequent part of our supper meal. On one occasion, I discussed this habit with Mom:

"Hi Mom, something smells great. What are ya fixing for supper?" "Meatloaf, mashed potatoes and gravy, and, oh yes, waxed beans."

"Waxed beans again, Mom?"

"Dad will be going shopping soon, and he wants us to use the last few cans in that case. Don't complain; the starving children in China would be happy to have a can of waxed beans to eat."

"Gee Mom, why don't we send them the last few cans and make them real happy."

"That's enough of that kind of talk. Dad works hard to put food on our table. If you don't eat the waxed beans I'm serving tonight, you won't have any homemade chocolate pie for dessert."

"I love waxed beans, Mom, pile 'em on and maybe I can have a bigger piece of your delicious pie."

"That's better; that's what I like to hear."

* * * * *

Monday was washday in the neighborhood. Backyard clothes lines – some pulley mounted and operated, while others strung for the day at ground level – were awash with fluttering and drying laundry.

Mom would do our laundry using a washboard and a galvanized tub and would wring each piece out by hand.

White shirts were boiled on the stove, in a copper colored smaller tub, and Mom would stiffen the collars and cuffs with dabs of starch. (Later in the decade, Dad bought an electric washing machine with an attached, hand-cranked wringer.)

As the clothes dried on the line, they were removed, folded, and replaced with a line full of additional laundry. The items that needed to be ironed were set aside. The next day, Mom would sprinkle them with drops of water and iron them using a heavy metal iron she heated and reheated on the hot stove surface.

During the winter months, some of the laundry on the line would freeze stiff before completely drying. We would maneuver stacks of those items through the doorway, and Mom would spread them around to dry in the warmth in the kitchen. Dad's one-piece frozen long johns were difficult to maneuver through the doorway until I realized that I could waltz them through. Mom didn't think that was very funny or, at least, she pretended that it wasn't.

* * * * *

During the week, I would take sponge baths while standing in the pantry, on a towel next to the sink, with a basin of hot soapy water at hand.

Saturday was the time to soak and bathe in the tub. Mom would draw the kitchen shades, and I would retrieve the round galvanized tub from its storage hook on the side porch. It was the tub that Mom used to do our laundry.

We would place the tub on a layer of towels near the stove, for easy access to the pots of steaming water. On cold winter nights, we would open the oven door to provide more heat to the immediate area, and I would drape my nightwear over the door to absorb the oven heat.

As siblings Lorraine and Gene grew into the toddler stage, they enjoyed the Saturday bath in the tub. I had outgrown it, and began taking baths in the full-sized tub – with hot and cold water faucets – in my paternal grandparent's home down the street. At other times, I would accompany Dad to the coal company shiftin' shanty, to take a shower.

* * * * *

The shanty, a perk provided to the underground workers by only a few companies, was a high-ceilinged, one-level structure located across the road from the mine slope where Dad worked. It contained a fairly large main room, with rows of back-to-back benches and a smaller, offset shower room that contained multiple shower heads that dispensed plenty of adjustable steaming hot water.

Each worker was assigned a space on the bench, where a pulley chain with an attached large bucket hung from the ceiling. While at work, the men would store a clean set of underwear and other items in the bucket and hang their outer garments on s-shaped hooks that rested on the bucket rim. At the end of the work shift, the men would shower, don their day wear, and store their work gear in the bucket. They would hang their outer work garments on the hooks, where they could dry and air out overnight, in the heated building. Finally, they would raise the bucket to the ceiling and secure the chain to the bench with a personal lock.

* * * * *

The other half of our duplex was occupied by Dad's sister, Aunt Lottie; her husband, Uncle Bozo, and his adult brother, "Goosy." The third residence in the duplex - two basement rooms - was occupied by Dad's cousin, Uncle Dudu, when he wasn't away serving his sentence, and his wife, Lil' Mary.

Besides being related in one fashion or another, we all got along really well. That was a huge relief, since we shared the four hole duplex outhouse divided by nothing more than thin panels and located in the far reaches of the backyard. We used and maintained one compartment, Aunt Lottie and her family the other, and Dudu and his wife used whatever compartment was available at their time of need.

Periodically, we cleaned our unit with a broom, bucket of water, and a cleaning agent and poured lime into the holes. Mom made a curtain, and Dad hung it on the door to cover the ¼ moon cutout. Mom claimed that the curtain was for decorative purposes, but Dad felt it was intended to keep people from peeking in while she was occupying the seat.

* * * * *

The outhouse was our daily activity and social center. On our way to and fro, we would exchange "how ya doin's" and weather-related comments. Quite often, we would exchange the following:

"What's up?"

"Not much, what's up with you?"

"Not much."

"That's good."

The outhouse atmosphere was not very conducive to having conversations while in simultaneous, but divided, occupancy. Comments were routinely disjointed by exertions and their associated or resultant sound effects. None of that deterred Uncle Bozo, who enjoyed and initiated our occasional conversations, wherein we would exchange very eloquent and informative lines, i.e:

(U.B. – Uncle Bozo/Jr. – me):

U.B. – Hey is that you over there, Junior?

Jr. – Yeh, is that you, Uncle Bozo?

U.B. – Yeh, how ya doing in school, Junior?

Jr. – Pretty good, Uncle Bozo. I got all 90s so far.

U.B. – That's great, Junior. A good education is an important thing to have in life, ya know. I wish that I didn't have to quit and go to work when I was your age.

Jr. – Yeh, that's what everybody tells me. How's the job comin' along, Uncle Bozo?

U.B. – Can't complain, Junior. I'm happy to have one during these tough times.

Jr. – Yeh, and how's everything else going, Uncle Bozo? How ya feeling these days?

U.B. – That's very nice of you to ask, Junior. I'm feeling a lot better now that I've gotten over the err...err...shits.

Jr. – Oh? Sorry to hear you had them, Uncle Bozo.

U.B. – We all get them at one time or another, Junior – some of us quite often – can't figure out why.

Jr. – Geez, thanks for telling me that, Uncle Bozo. You really didn't have to.

U.B. – No problem, Junior, just my way of telling you young ones what you can look forward to in life.

Jr. – Oh boy, thanks again, Uncle Bozo.

U.B. – Well, I've got chores to do. See ya, Junior.

Jr. – Yeh, see ya, Uncle Bozo, been nice chatting with ya.

U.B. – By the way, Junior, hope everything comes out well for ya. Ha ha ha.

Jr. – Same to you, Uncle Bozo. Ha ha ha.

While in solo occupancy, I'd occasionally watch a couple of spiders wrestle on the wall or watch one weave a web and trap well-fed insects. I would eventually scan the Sears' catalog and decide which pages I would tear out and use.

* * * * *

Visits to the outhouse in the winter, with the snowfalls and blasts of frigid temps and winds, was more of an inconvenience. We would clear a path the length of the long backyard through the snow, and scrape away the snow that blocked the door. Upon entering, I would remove my winter mittens and heavy jacket and proceed to fumble with the buttons on the back flap of my one-piece woolen union suit (**zymowe gaczl**). With teeth chattering and fingers getting cold, I wouldn't dally as I quickly scanned the catalog and reversed the process.

* * * * *

Pre-bedtime visits to the outhouse occasionally provided some intrigue.

During one short period of time, rumors circulated that a band of gypsies had been seen roaming the area. Mom was concerned and instructed me to be alert and come rushing back to the house if I heard any strange voices or noises in the alley. Mom stated, "I don't want any gypsies kidnapping my son." I told Mom that I didn't really believe that gypsies kidnapped young boys. Her response was typical: "Oh yeah, tell that to the couple from Mocanaqua, whose young son was kidnapped by gypsies when I lived there as a young girl."

I was on full alert as I cautiously walked down the path, scanning the area with the flashlight. Quietly, I snuck into the outhouse. I didn't hear any voices or noises, other than my heavy breathing. Afterwards, I raced back to the house, fearful of being grabbed from behind by a gypsy.

The gypsy rumor waned in a month or two, but my alertness continued for a while longer. After all, Mom's concerns were real.

* * * * *

One night, as I was about to head up the path, I noticed headlights coming up the alley. Sure enough, it was Dad. In the darkness, he didn't see me and, while he was maneuvering the car into the garage across the alley, I came up with the not so bright idea that it was a great time to see if I could scare Dad.

I crouched real low along a side of the coal shed, and when Dad came through the adjoining side gate, still crouched, I let out with a "yaaaah!" Dad let out some colorful language and shuffled his feet, and I sensed a whoosh and then another.

Realizing that I had probably gone a bit too far, I began shouting "Dad, Dad, don't be scared; it's only me, your son Breezy." After a moment or two of dead silence, Dad erupted in anger: "What in the hell prompted you to try to pull such a dumb and dangerous stunt?" he asked. He continued, "If my fists (and they were huge) had connected with your head, you'd now be lying there dead."

While we walked up the path together, Dad continued to angrily give me the mother of all lectures, and I began to fear that I was in really deep poo poo.

After we entered the house, my fears rose as Dad removed his leather belt. Motioning with his finger, he commanded me to "Come over here." Reluctantly, I complied as my eyes began to tear up. I was anticipating the pain I was sure I would soon feel from what would be my first whipping.

Dad extended his hands and the belt and sternly said, "smell the belt." I took a deep sniff, more so than I ever did in response to the wonderful aroma of Mom's hot, fresh out of the oven bread.

`"Do you smell it?" Dad asked.

"Yeh, oh yeh, Dad" I replied.

"That's good," Dad said, "the next time you'll feel it on your rear end; now go right to bed."

I felt that it wasn't the right time to tell Dad that I was feeling an urgent need to run back to the outhouse. Instead, I bounded up the stairs and used the lid topped potty, which was stored under the bed for emergency use. There were a couple more times that I crossed the line, and the outcome was the same, "smell the belt" treatment.

* * * * *

Whipping of young children was a form of punishment that was inflicted, with a leather belt or strap, by some parents. Others frowned upon or detested its use.

Dad and Mom were in the latter group. Mom, in disgust, occasionally recalled her family's former neighbor in Mocanaqua, a man who pet his dog after scolding it, yet, in the backyard, he unmercifully whipped his young children as they cried out in pain. Her dad intervened, stopped the man, and threatened him with physical retaliation if he ever did it again. Soon thereafter, the man moved his family to a different neighborhood.

* * * * *

It was fun growing up in our neighborhood, especially living on a paved street with a hill.

I had two similarly aged buddies living in adjacent homes and four similarly aged cousins sharing a duplex across the street. In our preschool days, our play was confined to our yards and porch. As we attended and progressed through our elementary school years, our play areas and circle of friends expanded. The street, with its light vehicle traffic, became a favored play area.

In the winter months, following a snow fall, we would ski down the hill on discarded curtain rods or race down on sleds, quite often doubled up because not everyone had sleds.

Our winter activities were not confined to the hill, nor were they dependent on frequent snowfall. During really cold periods, we would carry our ice skates as we skipped along the ties of the coal company feeder rail track on our way to the nearby frozen duck pond.

There, we would play tag or ice hockey, (using a discarded stick or branch and a crushed can as the puck. For more excitement, we would join the crack-the-whip line that was being formed by the older guys and girls (teenagers).

* * * * *

During the warmer months, we would ride up and down the street on bikes, wagons, roller skates, or homemade scooters. The latter were made using the short side of a 2 x 4, nailing a split skate to each end of the underside, and nailing a sturdy dynamite box (with attached homemade wooden handles) to the topside.

During these activities, we learned how to use Dad's patch kit and patched the bike tire inner tube flats and greased the wheel bearings on the bikes and skates so that we could go more easily and more smoothly.

Occasionally, we would salvage barrel hoops/rings. Some kids would propel them with sticks, but we had imagination. We would straighten a metal clothes hanger, bend the hook, and use the hook to propel and maneuver the hoop. We would walk it along the street and perform figure 8's and other improvised movements. (Decades later, someone produced a plastic tubular hoop and called it a "hula hoop." During that later fad, I showed my young daughters how to control and maneuver the hula hoops using the hanger technique.)

* * * * *

On Friday evenings, and more often during the summer vacation months, we would gather on the street. We were mindful of the fact that we would have to scurry home as the town's 9 p.m. whistle began to blare. We had an early warning when we heard the nightly eastbound mail plane fly overhead shortly before 9. There wasn't any curfew in our town, but the blowing whistle was a convenient reason for our parents to impose one on us preteens.

We would discuss local and national sporting events and results and play some games, including shooting marbles on our neighbor's dirt front walk.

As darkness descended, we would resorted to playing "hooper" our name for the childish game hide and seek. We would play in a yard because there weren't many good spots to hide on the street.

One night while playing in my yard, I hid behind the outhouse. I had no idea that Aunt Lottie was inside until she began fearfully asking, "Who's out there?" I didn't answer her, fearing that my buddies would hear and know where I was hiding, but they heard her and ran down and found me. In the ensuing din, she was shouting, "Who's out there?" and we quickly scattered.

* * * * *

During the mid-30s, as we were growing up and progressing through St. Mary elementary school, our play activities expanded and were dominated by our desire to play seasonal sports.

We participated in an after-hours basketball program at the school and played football and basketball in our alley. In the latter, we practiced two handset, and underhand foul shots, as we aimed at a thin wooden slatted fruit/vegetable basket that was nailed to a backyard barn or above a garage door.

We were instructed by our parents not to enter a yard to retrieve a ball without the permission of a family member who happened to be outside. Occasionally, an errant football would landed in our adjacent neighbor's yard as their three, slightly older daughters (Jania, Mania, and Frania) were in the yard. We would ask for their permission to enter, but they happily preferred to retrieve it. We would eventually tire of hearing them giggle and take turns trying to kick the football, and we would retrieve it and thank them for their effort.

* * * * *

Initially, we would play baseball across the street, on a small plot behind my grandparent's property. Soon, we gained access to a larger, virtually adjacent, coal company field after the debris was removed following a spectacular fire that destroyed the old mule barn. The night of the fire, Mom, Dad, and I were perched at the bedroom windows. We watched the flames and burning embers shoot up behind the houses across the street and the firemen wetting neighborhood roofs to prevent them from being ignited by the flying, burning embers.

Our new field contained a constricted outfield. Right field abutted a drainage creek, and left field abutted a coal company rail siding, where loaded coal cars were often parked prior to being hauled to market. With an occasional great swat, we'd hit the ball off the side of a coal car. Our new field also became our football field. It had a larger play area than the alley, and we didn't have to worry about a ball landing in a nearby yard, not even when we were trying to kick "booming spirals."

Everybody who showed up played. We didn't have enough players to field two full teams and usually played with a lesser compliment. Two of the oldest players would select their team members, and we laid down our own ground rules. They were as follows: Walks weren't issued; strikes weren't called; slowly count to 3 before rushing the "passer." We would play until we got tired or were called home.

* * * * *

Except for the after school basketball program, we played our athletic games unsupervised and without an adult coach. Our dads were at, or had just come home from, their hard jobs, and our moms were busy performing their household activities and rearing younger siblings. We learned how to play the games from our slightly older teammates as they critiqued us: "You're swinging too early/too late." "Catch the footballs in your hands," etc.

We shared all of our athletic equipment that we received as gifts on various occasions. We also acquired hand-me-downs. The latter included cracked bats and badly scuffed practice baseballs and footballs from older sibling high school athletes, and basketballs in a similar condition from the parish team on which the Bart Brothers (my uncles) played.

Black electrical tape was a cherished item that we would "borrow" from our Dad's toolboxes. After nailing a bat handle, we would wrap it in layers of tape. We would play our games on dirt and pebble strewn surfaces, and the balls didn't hold up too well. As the lacing and stitches on the footballs and baseballs broke and began to unravel, we would cover them with strips of tape. At times, we were swinging a black handled bat at a black and white baseball – in rare cases it was an all black ball. When a football bladder burst, we resorted to using a carnation condensed milk can. It fit perfectly in our developing hands, and allowed us to throw tight spirals.

* * * * *

On some Friday evenings in the fall, we would gather in "our" field and build a small bonfire. As the flames waned, each of us would throw new potatoes (*bindureks*) onto the burning coals. While waiting for them to cook, we would sit around and discuss sports events or express our dreams for the future. We're gonna be hot – shots on the high school teams; play basketball teams; play basketball on the parish team and match the legendary accomplishments of the Bart Brothers.; and oh yeah, play baseball for the powerful New York Yankees. By then, the potatoes were done.

We would retrieve them from the fire, blow on them as we juggled them in our hands, and, occasionally, chant "one bindurek" – "two binurek" – "three bindurek" – "four." Soon, we chewed through the charred skin and slowly savored the steaming potato. As the 9 p.m. whistle began blaring, we would kill the fire and head home.

Depression? What Depression? To us youngsters, this was the "normal" way of life, and we enjoyed it to the utmost.

CHAPTER SEVEN

MY FAMILY TRIPS

Prior to the mid-30s, Mom and Dad would walk to their various destinations in town. Mid-week, Mom would spend an afternoon visiting with her mother, in another part of town and often on Sundays, she and Dad would visit with her parents.

On Mom's weekday visits, she pushed me along in my carriage, and on their Sunday visits, Dad had the honors. When I was able to sit up, but not yet able to walk along with them, Dad bought a wagon and a sled to use depending on the weather conditions. He secured a dynamite box to both items and pulled me along as I sat on a blanket for padding. Later in the evening, they would time their departure for home so we wouldn't be near or abreast of the borough building when the 9 p.m. whistle was blaring.

* * * * *

To other local, but out of town destinations, they would ride the bus, and to reach more distant destinations they would ride a train. The longest train ride, an all-day ride, was to Pittsburgh to visit and attend special events with

Mom's sister, Aunt Gen (my godmother), her husband, Walter, and their similarly-aged daughter, Dolly.

* * * * *

In the summer of '34, a few weeks after completing first grade, I rode the train with Mom to Pittsburgh to spend some time with Aunt Gen and her family. Aunt Gen had requested Mom's help making a couple of thick feather pierzynas, but in essence it was an effort by Aunt Gen to help Mom cope with the death of my baby sister Elaine, who had died a couple of months earlier.

On the morning of the trip, I was anxiously anticipating the train ride as Dad drove us to our departure point at the northern terminus of the Pennsylvania Railroad in Wilkes Barre. My anticipation changed to excitement as we were boarding and I saw our large, header, coal-fired steam engine spurting steam and lazily belching smoke and cinders from its stack.

We sped south through the town of Mocannqua, where I hastily waved to Ciocia Juzia, Mom's uncle's wife, who was waving at the train from the backyard of the tracks. Ciocia Juzia enjoyed sharing her jars of powerful homemade "medicine" with visiting family members and was known for breeding chihuahuas that only responded to commands in Polish.

We continued along the banks of and criss-crossed the widening Susquehanna River, stopped at several stations along the way, and arrived at the station in Harrisburg, our state capital, where we had to transfer to a westbound train. An hour or so after arriving, we boarded and departed on a much longer train, pulled by a larger but similar steam engine. Our car was ventilated by ceiling fans and numerous open windows.

We eased onto a long bridge spanning the wide river, and soon our speed increased and the countryside seemed to be flying by. I enjoyed the scenery as we rolled through lush farmland and along wooded streams. My view was unobstructed, as long as the smoke pouring from the engine remained above the train. We stopped at several stations along the way and eventually arrived at the town of Altoona, the site of the railroad's sprawling manufacturing, maintenance, and repair shops.

Two huge and powerful steam engines were coupled to our train to help us go through the next exciting segment of our trip. Smoke, cinders, and steam were spewing from all of the engines as the train crawled up and around the scenic and famous horseshoe curve. Mom and I and the other passengers were gathered at the windows in awe of the scene wherein we could see both the front and back end of the train and could enjoy waving back at the people gathered along the curve.

We continued our pace up and over the mountain, where the engines began braking as we descended through a lone canyon to the valley town of Johnstown, the site of the destructive and devastating flood decades earlier. There, our helper engines were uncoupled and side tracked, to await and help the next eastbound train traverse the mountain.

We continued on the last leg of our trip and arrived at our destination in the evening, tired, sweaty, and grimy from the smoke and cinders that had infiltrated our car. I looked forward to our return trip.

* * * * *

When Dad bought his first car in the mid-30s, he soon grew to enjoy driving to various destinations. He drove Mom to Florida for a week long sightseeing trip and took her on shorter but similar trips to Niagara Falls, New York City, Philadelphia, and other regional sites. More often, however, we went on family vacations. In 1939, Dad drove Mom, me, and siblings Lorraine and Gene to New York City to spend a couple of days touring the World's Fair.

On occasion, we would rent a cottage at a local lake for a week, and were joined by Aunt Gen and her young family. At other times, we would vacation with them in Atlantic City or drive to Pittsburgh to visit.

The drive to Pittsburgh was a day long trek, and we would stop several times to have lunch or to take a break. It was a tiring ride, but it took less time and was cleaner than our previous passenger train method of transportation.

* * * * *

Sundays were the occasions for our family drives. We often drove to Macanaqua to visit with Mom's relatives. At other times, our destination depended on the season of the year and our combined desires. In the spring, we would drive through the countryside, happy to see the beginning signs of a new year of growth. In the fall, we would see dying cornstalks and leaves in various shades of red and yellow, and we'd stop at a farmhouse to buy pumpkins and apples for Mom to use to bake pies or other produce for her to preserve. In the winter, we would observe the inactive countryside blanketed with snow and we would seek out hillsides or frozen ponds for an afternoon of sledding or skating.

Our summer rides provided the most excitement and youthful activity. On occasion, we would go to Rocky Glen Amusement Park and enjoy the numerous rides, the games, and the funhouse. We went to Lake Idlewild, where Dad rented a boat and we fished for a while as Mom relaxed in the shade on a lakeside lawn, or to Chapman Lake, or Nay Aug Park, for an afternoon of swimming. The best rides were the ones to Lake Ariel and, occasionally, to Harvey Lake. Mom would pack a picnic basket with sandwiches, fried chicken, and potato salad, and it was a full day of activity that included swimming, enjoying the rides and games at the adjacent amusement park and ended as we watched the fireworks.

On one of the rides to Harvey Lake, I was awed to see, on display, a gangster, bullet-riddled car in which the gangster had been killed during the FBI's attempt to capture him. Alongside the car was a huge sign that read, "Crime does not pay," signed by J. Edgar Hoover, FBI Director.

As we were riding homeward, Dad had a knack of finding a route that would take us to our favorite Montdale Farm Dairy. We'd buy a double dip cone of their delicious homemade ice cream. The difficult part was deciding which flavors our taste buds desired most.

* * * * *

Dad was an avid sportsman and fan and enjoyed fishing and attending various professional sporting events. Usually once or twice a year, accompanied by brothers or friends, he would drive to a Canadian wilderness lake for a couple days of dedicated fishing. Several times a year, he and his brothers or friends would drive to New York City or Philadelphia to attend a professional football or baseball game or, on occasion, an Army-Navy football game. When I was about 9 years old, Dad began inviting me to come along.

* * * * *

On the fishing trips, one of Dad's accompanying friends would bring his slightly older son along. We camped at a lake in the Canadian wilderness and lived a backwoods lifestyle for a couple of days. We stored and chilled our food and beverages on blocks of lake ice that filled a pit and was covered by sawdust and a tarp. We slept in a tent, and I was occasionally awakened by the cry of a loon, and was sometimes frightened by the noises of other nearby wildlife. We two youngsters learned to scale and clean the fish and ice the ones to take home. Most of the day, we would row the boats for the elders, but we would also fish and catch northern and the prized and tasty walleyes.

* * * * *

The most impressive and memorable trips to a sports event were when Dad and I and one or two of his friends would attend an Army-Navy football game at the sold-out, 100,000-person capacity Memorial Stadium in Philadelphia, not only for the excitement and competitiveness of the game, but more so for the associated color and pageantry.

We would depart before dawn and by mid-morning would be passing by dew-covered grazing fields and estate lawns on the outskirts of the big city. Soon, we would ride along the banks of the Schuylkill River, past boathouse row, and past City Hall, capped by William Penn's statue.

We, along with most of the other fans, would arrive at the stadium well before kick-off time. I was struck to see the number of young and older women arriving in seemingly elegant fur coats, adorned with a large mum, team football pendants, waving to an Army or Navy pennant, and men arriving in suits and overcoats similarly adorned.

I was amazed by the precision of the corps of cadets and mid shipmen as they paraded into the stadium; by their on field formations; by the gusto and unison of their rallying cheers and fight songs; and the way in which they would finally lift their headgear as they expressed their final cheer, "Go Army" or "Go Navy." I soon realized the reason for their precision, as I noticed a cadet and a midshipman standing on the base of the tower atop the Stadium, snapping flag signals.

The half time show was a loose and humorous event as they paraded funny floats, engaged in hijinks, and, around the perimeter of the field, a cadet rode bareback on their mule mascot while midshipmen paraded their tethered goat mascot. The closing post game ceremony was solemn as the cadets and midshipmen, along with their assembled teams, stood bareheaded, with a hand over their heart, as they sang their alma mater. Emotions were evident in the faces of the seniors who had played in their last Army-Navy game.

* * * * *

The one-day trips to Yankee Stadium in New York City or to Shibe Park in Philadelphia were exciting, because I saw the legendary stars of that era for the Yankees, A's, and Phillies play baseball.

* * * * *

Decades later, after Dad retired, Dodo and I treated Mom and Dad to a few similar standout events. One Father's Day, I drove back home and took him to a nearby upstate lake (Quaker Lake) for some trout fishing. I brought along the bait (cheese, corn, and marshmallows) and rods. I anchored the boat over a rumored productive hole and Dad, a pure fly fisher for trout in his younger years, sat there in wonderment, thinking I was pulling a Father's Day joke on him by using this fishing technique. He watched as I threw some corn niblets into the water, rigged our rods for bottom fishing, and baited our hooks with corn niblets and small cubes of Velveeta cheese. In a matter of minutes, Dad was excited because we were repeatedly catching trout. A couple of hours later, Dad was all smiles and shaking his head in disbelief, as we were on shore and I was cleaning our combined limit of 16 trout. Mom greeted us when we arrived with a, "Did you catch anything?" Dad nonchalantly lifted the cooler lid, and, with hands clasped and an "oh my," Mom added, "That's what I like, men who not only catch fish, but clean ones at that."

* * * * *

I took Dad to see an Eagles football game, and he accompanied Dodo, me, and our daughter Janet to the 1976 Major League Baseball All Star Game in Philadelphia, where Dad watched his favorite player, Thurman Munson (New York Yankee catcher) perform. Thurman later died in a plane crash as he was practicing landings.

* * * * *

We also once took Dad and Mom to Philadelphia and sat next to the reviewing stand as we watched the string bands perform in the annual New Year's Day Mummer's parade. We were moved when we noticed the twinkle in their eyes as Mom and Dad recalled attending the same, but less elaborate, parade earlier in their marriage.

CHAPTER EIGHT

ELEMENTRY SCHOOL YEARS

In September 1933, three months prior to celebrating my 5th birthday and my sister Elaine's birth, some of my best neighborhood buddies started first grade at St Mary's Parochial Elementary School, a city block away from our home. I was devastated because I now had no one to play with. I wanted to join my friends, but Mom and Dad thought that I was too young to start school.

The next day, either Mom took me down to the school to let me see where my buddies were attending class, or I wandered off to school with my buddies for their afternoon session. Mom was summoned and came to retrieve me, but I was reluctant to leave.

On our way out, we met our pastor, Monsignor Szpotanski. He greeted Mom, asked about Dad, and asked if he could be of assistance. Mom told him of my desire to start school, and of her and Dad's concern regarding my age. Monsignor engaged me in conversation in Polish. I responded in kind as Mom and Dad had taught me to converse with my grandparents in their native tongue. He suggested that I join the class for the rest of the week, and said that Sister would evaluate my readiness to start school. Sister concluded that I was ready to continue my first grade. A decade later, I carried the cross and led Monsignor's funeral procession out of the church and to the cemetery grave site.

* * * * *

A year later, in September 1934, Dorothy enrolled in the first grade at Lincoln Elementary Public School, which was a first through sixth grade facility located in her section of town, some two blocks from her home. The teachers were primarily single women of various ages.

Dorothy easily made friends in school and in the neighborhood. She and her friends enjoyed riding bikes, roller skating, playing hop scotch, and jumping rope. During one of her playing sessions with her friends, her older brother Teddy came by and briefly stopped and observed her silly antics. He went into the house shaking his head and said, "That girl is a bird; she is a real Dodo bird." And that is how she became affectionately known to her friends and family as "Dodo Buza."

In the summers, she and an accompanying cousin or two would spend a few weeks at her grandmother's farm. They would help with the chores. They would swim in the pond. But, mostly, she would enjoy learning how to ride and then actually riding horseback.

* * * * *

St. Mary's was staffed by a contingent of about 20 Bernadine Sisters. They resided in a convent across the street, and they were impressive as they strode to school in brown woolen robes, starched white bibs, and black veils.

They had two basic rules. One, you behaved at all times; and, two, you did everything you could to learn what they were teaching. If you did not comply with those rules, it resulted in some appropriate punishment. It might even be physical and include a smack on the knuckles with a hard wooden ruler or a pointer. They did not hesitate to use it. They could be compassionate; they could be tough, or they could be mean. It all depended on you. It was your choice how they would treat you.

The nuns were excellent teachers. They taught us the three "R"s and the other usual elementary subjects. Some classes were conducted in English, while others were in Polish as we learned to read, write, and speak our ancestors' language.

I had some preschool training in speaking Polish. Mom and Dad tried to teach me some words so that I could converse with my grandparents. I really learned the Polish language, and I was able to converse quite proficiently with both sets of my grandparents in their native tongue. I became one of their favorites.

As part of our religious studies, we attended a weekly mass, either with our class or with the whole student body. The latter attended Holy Day Masses and various Lenten services, which included the Stations of the Cross.

CHAPTER NINE
ALTAR BOY CAREER

In September 1936, at the beginning of 4th grade, a number of my friends and I decided to become altar boys. We had to go through a training program. The Mass, prayers, responses, and hymns were all in Latin. We learned how to pronounce these Latin words and to understand their meanings. We then learned how to perform the services of an altar boy: The pouring of the wine, the timing of the ringing of the bells, how to hold a gold-plated paten under each communicant's chin as they received communion kneeling at the altar rail. To learn those services properly, we practiced with a nun who acted as the priest. We went through all the rituals, and when we finished that successfully, we were then designated an altar boy.

We were given two cassocks and a surplice. The black cassock was worn for the daily Masses and funerals. The red cassock was used for weddings, Sunday Masses, and high holy day services. Our names were sown on each cassock, and we were responsible for maintaining it and keeping it clean and well pressed. The surplices, made of white lace, were worn over the cassocks. They also had to be cleaned and pressed. My mother was great at that. She always said, "No son of mine is ever gonna have a dirt mark or a wrinkle on any of his alter service clothing."

* * * * *

A few months after I became an altar boy, a few of my altar boy friends and I were sitting out on the church steps, talking and just shooting the bull like kids at that age would. We all decided that we needed nicknames, and so we started selecting nicknames for each other. The first selection we made was pretty easy. My best friend and neighbor, Bernie, who was very short of stature, had an older brother about an inch taller who was known as "Big Spits." So it was easy; Bernie became "Little Spits." When it came to my turn, they figured that my nickname of "Junior" was adequate, but I just didn't like it. So for a while, we hassled about what my nickname should be. A nun came along, asked us what we were doing, and we told her. She asked if she could join in, and she is the one who came up with the name of Breezy. I don't recall what her reason was, but it sounded good at the time, and I became known to friends and family as "Breezy Bart."

* * * * *

Besides serving at the daily and Sunday Masses, we also served at weddings and funerals. I served at the weddings of many of my uncles and aunts as they were starting their married life. It was a joyous ceremony, and we also got tips for serving. Three altar boys served at a wedding. At one point, we would pass a glass dish around to all the ushers. They would put in coins of various denominations. We three shared that money. Sometimes we would get a dollar each. That gave us a little spending money.

* * * * *

At one point in my altar boy career, I participated in what was the first altar boy sitdown, I guess, in St. Mary's history. Because Frankie, Bernie, and I knew the wedding couple really well, the groom asked the ushers to put a little extra money for the altar boys in the plate. Low and behold: we had some dollar bills on that plate. After the Mass, when we went into the sacristy, the priest who conducted the ceremony told us that the money belonged to him. He took it and gave us each 10 cents. Well, that didn't sit too well with us. We sat there and griped about it and then decided that we were going to take some action. We went down to the rectory and asked the receptionist if we could see Monsignor Szpotanski. She told us he was busy in a meeting; we said we would gladly wait. She asked us why we wanted to see him. We told her we had a complaint against one of the priests. It didn't take Monsignor more than a few seconds to come out onto the porch, sit down with us, and ask, "What's the problem, boys?" We told him what had happened, and that Father had taken the money. Father was called out onto the porch to sit down with Monsignor and the three of us. He confirmed our story. At that point, Monsignor said to Father, "Let me have the money." Monsignor then took it and dished it out to us, apologized for the behavior of Father, and our sitdown was over.

* * * * *

Serving for funerals was a very traumatic experience. One altar boy would take the cross and go with the priest to participate in the service at the home of the deceased. There he would stand, holding the cross, as the family paid their last respects and closed the casket. This altar boy would then lead the procession into the church, down the aisle to the altar, where he would be joined by two other altar boys who also served during the Mass.

After the Mass was over, this altar boy would then take up the cross and lead the procession out of the church. When they would arrive at the cemetery, he would lead the procession to the grave site. There he would stand, holding the cross at one end of the casket as the priest went through the ritual prayers. He would continue to stand there and watch as the family said their farewell as the casket was being lowered into the grave. At that time, a really sorrowful Polish song was being sung: *Witay, Krilowo Nieba* (*Greeting to the King of Heaven*). Being one of the tallest altar boys, whenever I served at a funeral, I always carried the cross.

The first funeral Mass I served in was my maternal grandmother's funeral in October 1936, a few weeks after I became an altar boy. The first recollection I have of carrying the cross at a funeral was in 1938 at Dodo's mother's funeral Mass.

* * * * *

One Sunday a month, instead of serving Mass at church, I would accompany a priest out to the country to perform the Mass at a place called the Blakely Home, sometimes referred to as "the poor farm." Residents there were the elderly, the downtrodden, or the mentally challenged people. The residence buildings and the out buildings, which were painted a dull gray, were located out in the middle of farm land. It was supported by the county.

All of the residents there wore the same color clothing that was also furnished by the county. The residents not only lived there, they also worked there. They either worked in the kitchen, cleaned the buildings, or worked on the farm growing the food that fed them. Some of these residents had mental problems. Some were just too old, or poor or didn't have any family to help them. Some were actually abandoned by their families who couldn't afford to take care of them. At times, they walked around by themselves, or in pairs, in the same type of clothes, deep in their own thoughts. It was tough for a young boy at my age to realize how brutal life could be for certain people.

During the 30s Mom's sister-in-law and brother-in-law worked at the facility, the former as a cook, the latter as a medical staff aide. They told us many a story about the conditions and the life experienced by these residents. The most depressing story concerned the mentally impaired residents who at times became physically abusive. During such an incident the medical staff would dump them into a tub of ice to shock them out of their condition. If that didn't work, they would temporarily place the patients in straitjackets and place them in individual padded cells where they could do no harm to themselves or other patients.

* * * * *

Every January and February, the priests would visit every parish home in Dickson City. They did this for two reasons. One was to perform a census, and the other was to get their annual donation to the church. The priest was accompanied by a church custodian and an altar boy who carried the holy water in a dispenser. The priest would use that holy water to bless the home. He also carried a little metal piggy bank to hold any contributions. These visits were done during the week, regardless of the weather. On many days it was really cold, and on some it would be snowing.

I accompanied the priest a few times during these annual visitations. It was the height of the Depression, and it gave me an opportunity to see how people lived.

When we first entered the home, the custodian would use the piece of chalk to write over the front door:"19+K+M+B+36, or whatever the year was and that was to signify the visit of the three kings. When we walked further into the home, only the rooms that were being actively used that day were being heated; the doors to the parlor or dining room were closed to preserve heat.

When the priest finished with the blessing of the home and the taking of the census, we were generally offered a plate of soup from a pot that had been simmering on the stove. One particularly freezing day, a woman offered us pea soup. I didn't like pea soup, but it turned out to be the best pea soup I had ever tasted. That night, when I got home, I told my Mom that I had eaten some really good pea soup. She looked at me with hurt in her eyes, and said, "How can you say that, after all the times that I made pea soup for you, and you never even wanted to taste it." After that I made sure that whenever Mom made pea soup I ate it. At the end of a visitation day, I would empty my piggy bank and find up to a dollar in coins.

* * * * *

In 1943, when I was a sophomore in high school, I was still an altar boy. I went with the priest on the annual visitations to parish homes that we had visited during the Depression. The doors were now open, to all of the rooms, and the homes were well heated. On the parlor walls there were pictures of their children, in various military uniforms; in the front window, there was a little flag. It had a silver star for each member of the family who was in the service, and a gold star for each member who had died while serving. Occasionally, we would see a decorated Christmas tree, standing in the parlor to be seen by one of their children due home soon on furlough.

* * * * *

There was more to St. Mary's than just being an altar boy. At all grade levels in the school, they taught you how to read, write, and speak Polish. I had some preschool training in speaking Polish. Mom and Dad tried to teach me some words so that I could converse with my grandparents. During this course, I really learned the Polish language, and I was able to converse quite proficiently with both sets of grandparents in their native tongue. I became one of their favorites.

On the first of May every year, there was a combined family and school picnic. It was called a Myitca. The picnic was held about a half a mile up the side of a mountain at a spot we called the cold springs. This area was developed and maintained by the Boy Scouts, who used it for various camping activities. At the lower area, there was a very small parking area with a stream running through it with bridges over the streams made by the Scouts. The bridges had rocks for hand rails and painted stones. On the other side of the hill, there was a pipe with continually flowing cold spring water. On the upper level, which was a much larger area, there were fields where children would play games, and the tree and wild dogwoods were blooming.

It was an all-day affair and started early in the morning, when you would see families walking up the mountain carrying picnic baskets. The highlight of the day was when word would spread that Monsignor was on his way. All the children would run down to the lower level, and Monsignor would pull into that little parking area in his big 4-door Buick with a big cigar in his mouth. He would get out of the car to the screaming and yelling of the children and would reach into the back seat of that car and would pull out bags of candy and distribute them to the group. He enjoyed watching the children diving for the candy and screaming and having fun. At the end of the day, everyone would be worn out, but fortunately the walk back home was all downhill.

* * * * *

At the height of the winter, after school was let for the day, we would use the facilities at St. Mary's to play our winter sports and games. Basketball teams were organized at the various grade levels, and one day a week we would play in the main hall. Other times, we would go down to the lower level auditorium and there we would play floor shuffle board or ping pong or toss rubber rings.

* * * * *

When I turned 12 years old and was in 8th grade, I was hired for my first paying job. I worked at our local bakery on Friday nights for 3 to 4 hours. I would clean the vats that the bakers used to mix the dough for baking rye breads, pies, and doughnuts; clean and grease the baking pans; coat doughnuts with icing or sugar, and fill numerous trays of doughnuts with various fillings. The most common fillings were Boston cream and jelly, and they happened to be my favorites.

As I opened the gallon-sized cans one night, I continually taste tested and verify the fillings' freshness. Both passed the test. After filling the insertion bags, I determined the proper squeeze pressure to insert the adequate amount of filling by squirting some into my mouth, and also, while filling the doughnuts, I continued the sample testing. Soon, I wasn't feeling too well, and the feeling became worse by the time my work was done. I took home a loaf of warm rye bread that night rather than the filled doughnuts that were offered, and it was a long time thereafter before I again had a desire for a cream- or jelly-filled doughnut.

* * * * *

In the early part of 1941, it was announced that the tax collector position, the most financially rewarding political office in town, would become vacant at the end of the year. The victorious Democratic candidate in the upcoming May primary would be assured of victory in the November general election due to the overwhelming Democratic voter population in town.

Dad decided to file his candidacy for that office. Dad's political colleague, the police chief, who was nicknamed "Cowboy," and who Dad had previously and successfully nominated for a position on the police force and subsequent promotion to chief, also decided to file his candidacy for the same office in the Democratic primary. These two strong-willed, political power brokers, both with drive and determination and with relatively comparable physical stature, would lock horns in a mammoth primary political battle.

The campaign in our town was typically divisive, expensive, and down and dirty. One late weekend evening, I was walking home from an early movie. I turned the corner onto Carmalt Street, about 2 ½ blocks from home. At the next intersection, there was a vacant corner lot. I could see that it was well-lit that evening and that plenty of hooting and hollering was going on. I came to the corner and stopped to see what was happening. The lot was packed with men. A few I recognized from our neighborhood, but more were men for whom my Dad had gotten jobs after family pleadings during the recent Depression. At the other end of the lot was an elevated platform surrounded by beer kegs and whiskey bottles. It was adorned with lights, flags, a loudspeaker, and a huge political banner of Cowboy. He was giving his political speech as the crowd nodded and appropriately booed and cheered as they raised their beer and whiskey mugs to their lips.

I stood there listening and soon realized that he was criticizing and flat out lying about my Dad, and the family, in vulgar words that I had barely begun to understand at my age. I found myself feeling various emotions. I wanted to shout at Cowboy, "Stop lying about my Dad; you know he is a good man!" I wanted to shout to the crowd, "Don't believe these lies, especially those of you for whom my Dad has recently gotten jobs!" I found myself fearful that some of these men would recognize me and was afraid of what they might do or say to me in their drunken state.

I ran home, past the high school where in a prior year an on-duty town police officer had been shot dead while trying to break up a fight between political opponents at an ongoing open board meeting. I told my Mom what I had seen and heard. As she approached to hug me, she shook her head in disgust and said, "I can't for the life of me understand what pleasure men get from politics. I hope you never run for office."

On election night, after the votes were counted, Mom and I received word that Dad had narrowly lost the election and that he would be home later. We were told to lock the doors and not allow anybody in.

In a short while, we heard vehicles with their horns blowing coming up our street. Mom and I ran upstairs to close the windows so the noise wouldn't wake Lorraine and Gene. As we were shutting the front windows, the caravan, led by a big stake-bodied truck, stopped in front of our house. Cowboy stood on the truck bed surrounded by his minions of drunken supporters. They were shining spotlights at our windows as he was cursing at and calling Dad out.

We crouched on the floor, hugging each other. Mom was crying, with a look of fear on her face, worrying what they might do next. Finally, the caravan moved on. Dad, with urging from Mom, retired from his active political career.

About a year and a half after taking office, Cowboy was driving home from the mountains, at night, during a blackout drill, and his car hit a bridge abutment. His recent victory ended Dad's political career, and now his political career and natural life were ended. About two years earlier, I had stood at one end of that lot while he stood on a raised platform on the other end critiquing Dad. Now I held the cross at one end of his casket as the priest recited the final prayers.

In June, I graduated from St. Mary's and was looking forward to entering the public high school system. Meantime, Dodo was finishing seventh grade (first junior high level).

CHAPTER TEN

HIGH SCHOOL

In the summer of 1941, World War II was well underway. In the Pacific, Japan was conquering countries in Southeast Asia and island nations in the southwest Pacific and was engaged in a prolonged war with China. In Europe, Hitler's troops, with the support of Mussolini's Italian forces, were on the march. They had conquered, most, if not all, of the countries in Europe and Africa and were now conducting bombing raids against England in an attempt to destroy their military capabilities.

There were two attitudes about the war. One, especially by the people who remembered the horror and casualties experienced in WWI just a couple of decades earlier, said, "Let stay out of it; it's the European's war, and we shouldn't get involved." The other attitude was, "We have to step in and help England survive or we'll be the next to be attacked."

Our factories were gearing up and producing the war material that was needed by England to help them survive as their production capabilities were being destroyed by the German bombing raids. The increased manufacturing activities were the catalyst that ended the Great Depression.

People began leaving Dickson to go to Bridgeport, Connecticut; or Buffalo or Binghamton, New York to get employment at the different war producing factories. Every Friday night, carpools would arrive from those cities, and every Sunday night they would depart.

As production demands increased and the facilities were operating around-the-clock, more of our residents were departing to those cities and, soon, many of them with their families permanently relocated to those areas. Dodo's brother Vince and his wife Dorothy, sister Belle, and Uncle Adam and his family permanently relocated to Connecticut, while brother Ted relocated on a temporary basis pending his induction into the military service.

* * * * *

In September, I enrolled in the 9th grade at our local junior high school. We had morning and afternoon sessions, with about an hour break for lunch, and most of the students went home to eat. This was the first time I had attended classes with public school students and it was an opportunity to make a lot of new friends.

In October, my Grandfather Szczypanski died, three days shy of the fifth anniversary of Grandma's death. A few weeks later, on Armistice Day, as my 13th birthday was nearing, we moved from Carmalt Street to Mom's family home, at 642 Boulevard Avenue. We bought the home following Grandma's death to relieve Grandpa of the taxes and maintenance costs and to give him the comfort and security of living there for his remaining years. We finally had our own home and I had the adjoining Polonia Park and River to explore with my new friends. Most of all, we had central heat, hot water, and indoor plumbing, the latter ending my daily treks to the outhouse.

* * * * *

Mom's youngest sibling, Aunt Babe (21), had resided with her dad and remained to live with us. During my previous visits to the family home, she had treated me as her baby brother and showered me with affection. Soon, I felt the joy of having a resident older sister as she insisted that I refrain from calling or referring to her as "Aunt Babe." Together, we would wash and dry the dishes and cooking utensils from the evening meal and soon shared other household chores as it became obvious that Mom was pregnant and soon gave birth to my brother, Ron, born in August 1942.

On occasions, we would talk about her experiences at her job and mine at school, the character and traits that girls found most desirable in male counterparts, and the traits I should look for in any girl I considered dating. With Mom critiquing, Babe taught me the dance steps to the

Polish dances and the big band modern music, including the "jitterbug," a dance that Mom didn't really fathom as real dancing.

Babe and I developed a close sister-brother relationship, and in 1945, when I was 16 years old, I felt honored to serve as the best man at her marriage to Chester Novack and again a few years later as the godfather to their only child, my cousin Ken. Thereafter, I would often visit them, and we would share a meal or, more often, a delicious cake that they were both equally expert at baking. Decades later, in our senior years, I sat behind Babe at a family event and, leaning forward, complimented her on her youthful appearance, especially her hair's original jet black color, but then, her acknowledging and appreciating nod and smile, turned to a look of shock and disbelief as I asked, "So why are you dying the roots gray?"

* * * * *

On Sunday, December 7, 1941, we were visiting Mom's relatives in Mocanaqua, as we often did. It is a small, neighborly, sleepy, river town on the east bank of the Susquehanna River, across from its twin city, Shickshinny, and over the mountain from nearby Glen Lyon. My cousin Zaki and I were playing football outside when we saw people come out onto the porches, shouting across the street to one another and women crying. We ran home to find out what was happening, and we saw the women in our family crying. The men were upset and told us that the Japanese had attacked us at Pearl Harbor and that war was imminent. We didn't know where Pearl Harbor was and were scared, but we calmed down slightly when we were told it was in the far off Pacific Ocean.

The next few days, as Congress was declaring war at President Roosevelt's request against Germany, Japan, and Italy, long lines were forming at the recruiting offices. Young men who, only a few years earlier, had lined up to obtain government surplus food to feed their families were now lining up to sign up and enlist in the military and defend the country.

In the ensuing months and years, these young men and lads stood in mess hall chow lines and in lines to receive various medals denoting heroic actions. Sorrowfully, some would lay in a line of caskets in the process of being shipped home, where in finality, their caskets would lead the procession line of mourners to the cemetery for burial with full military honors. I felt honored and was often teary-eyed as I carried the cross at some of these funerals, especially for the ones whom I knew well.

All through my elementary school years, the country had fought a Depression, and now in my high school years, we would be fighting a war.

* * * * *

In late winter of my freshman year, I finally worked up the nerve to ask one of my cute classmates if she would like to accompany me to the movies. She agreed, but told me she wasn't allowed out alone and would have to bring along her girlfriend. When I approached them at the theater, I extended my hand to her girlfriend and said, "Hi, I'm Breezy Bart," and she took mine and said, "Hi, I'm Dodo Buza." I immediately recognized the name of the 9-year-old girl I had watched sitting at her mother's funeral several years ago, but did not recognize her. After all, we had grown quite a bit in the interval and had recently become teenagers.

After a couple of weeks, Dodo began to feel like she was a third wheel, so I introduced her to my buddy Frank. For several months, the four of us would go to the movies once a week. My girlfriend soon realized that she was at least a year older than me, and one night told me that she thought it was time that she dated older guys. Now I would join Frankie and Dodo at the movies, and it wasn't too long before I realized I was the third wheel. Dodo and Frankie were to date for the rest of our high school career. The three of us continued to be best friends.

* * * * *

For the next few years, the topics that dominated our life were the war progress, resident casualties, and home front and school activities. Our factories were now running at full capacity and were being converted from civilian to military production. Instead of cars or other big ticket items coming down the assembly line, there were tanks and jeeps and ships and planes. More people were leaving the area now to work in these war production plants, and many would relocate permanently.

Young men and senior students were enlisting so that they could serve in the military branch of their choice. Others were being drafted. Several times a month, hundreds of people would gather at the local train station. They would shed tears and wave goodbye to our young friends and relatives who were leaving to report for active duty. My Aunt Babe and I went out to Pittsburgh to wave goodbye to my Uncle Joey as he departed for service in the Army.

In the Pacific, our Navy surprised the Japanese Navy off the island of Midway, and we were able to sink four of their aircraft carriers. This was the first major battle that we had won in the Pacific. We had now slowed the Japanese momentum, and we were able to start going on the offensive.

Our troops were now fighting and would eventually drive the Germans out of Africa, thus opening up a southern route for a future invasion of Europe. Other American troops were being staged in England for a future invasion from the west. A large portion of our Air Force was deployed to England, and from there they were conducting nightly raids on strategic targets in Europe. More so, they were concentrating on bombing the war production facilities in Germany. Hundreds of our biggest bombers would participate in an individual raid. Casualties started to mount, and now we were occasionally having young men being returned home for burial with military honors.

On the home front, rationing of goods and food was our big contribution to the war effort. Items that were rationed included butter, sugar, flour, and various meats, along with gasoline and tires. Each month, we would receive books of stamps for the family, and these stamps allowed us to buy whatever product was represented on the stamp in the quantity designated. Gasoline rationing was accomplished through the use of coupons which were designated either class A, B, or C, depending on whether the vehicle was being used in the war effort, commercial business, or for pleasure. Each class allowed a certain number of gallons to be purchased. What a turn of events! During the Depression, the people didn't have the money to buy the food or the goods that they needed, and now they had the money, but the food and the goods were rationed.

* * * * *

Six months after we moved into our new home, the Lackawanna River flooded. With our house on the lowest lot in the neighborhood, the water line reached the foundation of the home, and water seeped into our basement. Mom and I were bailing and dumping it down the sink, while Dad was at a town in the valley, rescuing people from the flooding. Our garage was under one to two feet of water, and many of Mom's mementos and family albums that were yet unpacked were floating in the water. We spent months cleaning up the debris and eventually raised the level of our backyard one to two feet.

* * * * *

In 1943, I was still an altar boy and occasionally accompanied the priest on the annual visitation to parish homes, including some that I had visited during the Depression. The doors were now open at all the rooms, and all of the rooms and homes were well-heated. On the parlor walls there were pictures of their children in various military uniforms. In the front window there was a little flag with a silver star for each member of the family who was in the service and a gold star for each member who had died while serving. Occasionally, we would see a decorated Christmas tree being held to be seen by one of the children who was due home soon on furlough. I carried the cross at the funeral of some of the gold star heroes.

On March 21, 1943, my good buddy, Uncle Joey, died of an alleged heart attack after being rushed to the base hospital. He had stayed at our home during a recent furlough, and had appeared to be in really good health. He was stationed at the Army air base at Keeslerfield, Mississippi. Now we had a gold star in the window.

Within a few weeks, Joey's beneficiary, Aunt Babe, received a letter from a woman in Mississippi whose last name was Syke. She claimed, without any evidence, that she and Joey had been secretly married some months prior, and she was demanding his military life insurance proceeds. Babe responded and explicitly told her where to go, and she was never heard from again.

In March 1943, Monsignor Szpotanski died. He had been our pastor for over 20 years and was the one who, a decade earlier, had convinced Mom that I was ready to start first grade. Now I was carrying the cross at his funeral, leading him to his final resting place. About a week later, I again carried the cross, and led the Reverend Dominiak, our new pastor designee, into church for his formal appointment ceremony. Thereafter, my mother always proudly said, "My son led one priest out, and the new one in."

I was now taller than most of the priests. My Grandma Bart frequently told me that I looked like a real priest up at the altar. She would encourage me again to become one. I would always reply, "Nie mie, Babcia; ja kocham dziewczyny." Translated: "Not me, Grandma; I love girls."

* * * * *

During our junior school year, one of our big activities was the selling of war bonds. They were nothing more than government-issued savings bonds. They were sold in various denominations, like $25 or $50, or whatever higher value dollars you wanted. The $25 bond would cost you $18.75. Not everybody was able to buy one for the full price, so you could buy 10¢ stamps and place them in a booklet until it was filled. The full booklet amounted to $18.75, and you could then turn it in and get a $25 war bond.

Besides playing in sports, I was also playing an accordion in the high school orchestra and, twice a week, we would have our rehearsals. I would carry my accordion back and forth from home. It was a half mile each way, and it seemed like both ways were uphill. With all the activities I was involved in, I was just too busy to have any girlfriends, even on a casual basis.

Our social activities mostly took place in groups. We were starting to have sweet 16 birthday parties. At one of the parties, it was my turn, and I gave a girl my best kiss. She stepped back and said, "You kiss that good and you're an altar boy?" When it was her turn, she picked one of my buddies. I guess I just wasn't that good. It was about this time that I decided it may be time to retire. Not long thereafter, I retired as an altar boy.

In the winter, we would go ice skating, skiing, or tobogganing. In the summer, we would go swimming or to picnics at the cold springs, or we would just hike over the mountains. Dodo, Frankie, and I would be at all of these social activities, and our friendship continued to grow. In fact, in my junior year, I was hospitalized for a few days with a back injury, and one afternoon, Dodo and her girlfriend, a classmate of mine, came up to visit me.

* * * * *

On the 6th of June, 1944, as my junior high school year was coming to an end, our troops invaded Europe in what has famously become known as D-Day. During the next twelve months, the war really reached a crescendo. In the Pacific, we were doing more and more island jumping, and were now getting closer and closer to Japan. In Europe, our troops were on the march. We liberated Paris, and we liberated many of the countries that Hitler had occupied. Friends and former students were now receiving medals. Casualties really started to mount. It seemed like every week one of our young service people was being returned home for a military funeral.

In addition to our friends, we had family members who were also serving. Dodo's brother Teddy was a bomb crew member in the Pacific and had participated in at least 26 bombing missions. She had two future brothers-in-law who were in the Navy, and she had several uncles who were in the Army. I had uncles serving in the Army, Dad's youngest brother Walter and Mom's cousin from Maquinocqua, Stanly, serving in the Army. In January of 1945, we learned that Stanly had been killed in the Battle of the Bulge over the Christmas holidays. Now our family earned its second military burial and another gold star in the window. That was the last major battle in Europe and, after that, it was a race to see who got to Berlin first, the Russians or us.

In my senior year in high school, I was still a member of the orchestra, and I was honored then to be elected the class vice president. I was also named a starter on the varsity basketball team. We had a really good team that year. Our home games were played in a compact basement gymnasium where the baskets hung on opposing walls. The players would sit against one wall, a side wall on the court, and the other side would be where the fans were seated. Over one half of the court the ceiling was low, and on the other half it was even lower. We used that to our advantage. We would put the tallest three men up front on defense, and when the other team would come down, we would make them shoot against the lower part of the ceiling during the first half. They would try to shoot over our extended arms. Invariably, their shots would start hitting the ceiling, and that would psyche them out for the rest of the game. Out of all our home games, we only lost one all year. They were played in the afternoons. Our away games were played at night, and all of our games were played in front of packed houses. Dodo was now one of my loudest fans.

We continued our war bond rallies that year, and at the various rallies, students would get up and do various skits for entertainment. At one particular rally, my classmate and friend Bernie, who stood at most, five foot six, if that, and I, put on a skit in which we imitated Bud Abbott and Lou Costello. We performed their baseball routine and a couple other routines, and we had the students just roaring. That year, the senior high school sold over forty-one thousand dollars in war bonds.

Our group social activities were still going strong, but now we added dancing and bowling to the top of the list. Occasionally, on Tuesday, Thursday, or Sunday, we would dance at the pavilion in Palonia Park, to records of the big bands. A couple times a month, we would have a teeny bobber dance at the Borough Hall. The boys would come dressed in casual pants and shirts and casual jackets. The girls would come with their sweaters, skirts, bobby socks, and penny loafers. Across from Borough Hall was an establishment owned by the Towers family. It was a combination tavern, restaurant, back room with booths, and a juke box for dancing, a pool room, and a basement bowling alley. We would avail ourselves of all those activities, except for the tavern, and we would shoot pool, or have a bowling league of our own. Afterwards, we'd be upstairs in the back room dancing or having an ice cream soda, French fries, or delicious, homemade hamburgers. I'd encounter Dodo; she would be there with a friend or two, and we'd sit, chat, and share all of the goodies. We would talk just like two good old friends. Our friendship seemed to be growing.

There was other significant social event that happened that year. On December 16, 1944, my friends, with the help of my mother, threw me a surprise sweet sixteenth happy birthday party.

Our prom was scheduled to be held at St. Mary's hall in February. Frank and Dodo were going, along with a lot of my other friends who were paired up with girls. I was undecided, because I really didn't have anybody who I especially wanted to ask to go. My Uncle Iggy and his wife, Ann, came to the rescue. They arranged for me to meet Ann's niece, Lillian, a senior at Scranton Technical School, on the night that we played our basketball game there. After the game, there was a dance, and she was to come up and introduce herself to me. She did. She was very cute and could dance really well. I had my date for the prom. Another good friend of mine, also named Frank, invited a neighbor, Adeline, a junior in school, to go to the prom with him, and she agreed. Adeline was a very intelligent, attractive, and serious girl. Prom nights are usually fun, but ours turned out to be really funny.

My Dad's pre-war car had a quirk to it. Whenever it would get really cold, the back door latches would freeze, and there would be no way to get the doors open. On prom night, it was bitterly cold. When the prom ended, Lillian, with my friend Frank and his date, Adeline, decided to drive down and join our friends at Thomas' barbecue joint.

When we went to get into the car, sure enough, the back doors were frozen. We had a problem on our hands, but we easily solved it. We decided that Adeline would sit in the back seat, and we'd help her over the front seat. Frank, Lillian, and I would sit in the front. We had some fun getting Adeline into the back seat of that car. When we got to Thomas', Adeline, with her hair and gown askew, looked at us and said, "Just bring mine out here to the car; I'm not going through that again." We went in and got our food and there we sat, the four of us in the car, just having a ball, laughing and eating. When we got back and dropped Frank and Adeline off, she got out and wasn't very happy when she said good night to us. She just didn't have much of a sense of humor.

Lillian and I dated for the next several months. I was very active and busy, and so was she. We lived towns apart; her family didn't have a telephone, and communications were difficult. Finally, that summer, we drifted apart.

In the spring, our faculty determined that we would perform the operetta, *The Forrest Prince.* All of the students were encouraged to participate. We ended up with a cast of about 100 students, and the ones who weren't actively in the cast made the scenery, sold tickets, and sold ads for the program. We had about 40 Cossack dancers in the cast, equally divided between boys and girls. We had ballerinas and court jesters. Some had singing roles, and I had the role of the king. Dodo was a junior at the time, and was our prompter. She basically ran our rehearsals. She'd give us our directions and cues as she followed the script she had in front of her. On the night of our performance, she was in the orchestra pit, and she was just whispering our directions and cues as they were needed. The performance was sold out. We all had fun, and it was a hit.

As my senior year was rapidly coming to an end, we released our yearbook. We deemed it an honor to dedicate our book to our alumni who were in the service of our country, and we paid special honor to our alumni who had paid the supreme sacrifice, including my Uncle Joey. Six of my thirty-four fellow classmates had their pictures in the yearbook in military uniform, since they had already left before graduation to enlist in the armed forces. After we graduated, more of us, including some girls, enlisted or were drafted for two- to three-year tours of duty. In fact, one of my fellow classmates made the Marine Corps his career.

On the eighth of May, 1945, roughly a month before we graduated, Germany unconditionally surrendered, and the war in Europe was over. What a nice early graduation present.

Graduation night, we filed onto the stage in front of a packed house. Spirits were on the rise since the unconditional surrender of Germany. Our class president, my good friend, Joe, delivered the commencement address, and he paid special tribute to the alumni, especially those who were in the service. He also paid tribute to our parents and to our teachers, some of whom were also in the service. Joe and I had been classmates at St. Mary's; we served together as altar boys, and now we were graduating together as class officers. (Joc went on to be ordained as a priest in the Jesuit community. He studied and taught theology in Rome, and he would go one to author and have published at least three books on theology.)

Missing on the stage that night were my six fellow classmates who were already in the service. Missing in the audience was my mother, who was at a local hospital, after just delivering my baby sister, Andrea. But her seat wasn't empty in the audience; a whole bunch of my aunts from both sides decided that they would fill in for her, and they accompanied Dad to the graduation.

Later that night, I drove up to the hospital in my cap and gown, and when I went in, the nurses looked at me in surprise. I explained to them what was happening, and they quickly led me to the door of the ward that my mother was in. It was a ward with eight beds, four on each side. We opened the door. There was a night light on. I whispered, "Hey, Mom," and eight women answered me. My mother said, "No, no, that's my son, Breezy; he's graduating tonight," and all the lights went on, and everybody began tearing up. I went over to Mom and said, "Mom, here's what I looked like tonight," and she was real happy to see me. We exchanged hugs and shed some tears, and she said, "I am so happy you came, but don't stay too long, for tonight's the night to enjoy with your friends; it will be your last night as a group. Have fun."

When we as a class split up that night, we vowed that we would hold reunions every five years, and we did. And in 2005, at our sixty-year reunion, 30% of us attended, and we were pleasantly surprised to find that 60% of us were still alive.

Our troops were now starting to return from Europe, while others were being diverted to the Pacific theater, to prepare for the invasion and ultimate defeat of Japan. In late July, President Truman was advised that an invasion of Japan would result in hundreds of thousands of American casualties. He then issued an ultimatum to Japan, calling for their unconditional, immediate, and complete surrender. Japan refused the ultimatum, and on August 5, 1945, a single American plane dropped a single bomb on a city in Japan. Tens of thousands of people were killed on impact, and many more thousands would die shortly thereafter. Again, the President issued the ultimatum to Japan, and again they refused. On August 9, another bomb was dropped on Japan with the same deadly results. Five days later, Japan surrendered unconditionally. The war was over, and the celebrating began.

St. Mary's annual parish picnic had been underway that week, and that particular night it became the magnet for the valley celebration. We were sitting and celebrating on our front porch, roughly five homes away from the main entrance to the park. We were amazed as we watched Boulevard Avenue and the surrounding streets become a traffic jam. People drove as close to the park as they could get, and then parked, abandoned their cars, and then danced their way up the street or sidewalk, singing patriotic songs. We joined in. Many stopped to join us on our porch, and we just watched as the crowd assembled. At the park, it was a sea of humanity; people were dancing on the dirt fields. Others were trying to get to the refreshment stands, and still others were lined up, trying to get into the tent where beer and liquor were being served. The celebrating went on until the wee hours of the morning.

Dickson City, had a pre-war population of about 14,000 people that rapidly declined during the war, had 2,100 of its sons and daughters fight in the war, and 64 of them paid the ultimate sacrifice.

* * * * *

(Later on, that WWII fighting generation was recognized as the greatest generation. Right up there with them should be their parents. They had come from foreign countries to escape tyranny, and had come to this country to enjoy the freedoms, and opportunities that were offered here. They raised their children through a depression, and then saw these children go to war, fight, and give up their lives to free the countries from which they had come. They didn't ask or demand food stamps or welfare or unemployment checks or Medicaid or Medicare. They felt that you worked for everything you needed and wanted, and you served when the country needed you.

When they or their family members got sick, they tried all the home remedies they knew, and if those remedies failed, only then would they go to a doctor. If they didn't have the money to pay the doctor, they would barter, or they would pay them later, or the doctor would just overlook the bill. They were determined, hard working, moral people, and they had a dream of freedom and a better life, if not for themselves, then at least for their children. These traits made this country great.

It was a privilege to have lived in and to have witnessed that era of our history.)

CHAPTER ELEVEN
COLLEGE DAYS

In late summer 1945, the country entered an extended transition period. The Depression was no longer a worry in people's minds. The war was over, and we were moving into peace time. Our manufacturing facilities were now converting back to civilian production. Big ticket items like cars and refrigerators were again coming off the line. The rationing was suspended, but many items were still in short supply. It was not unusual to see a block-long line of women trying to get into a store that had just received a shipment of nylon stockings. There were often similar lines in front of cigar stores, as people lined up to get cigarettes which had just been delivered. There were also often lines in front of the candy store to get the Hershey bars that had just come in.

Automobiles were in demand, and it would take several months before the car you had ordered would be delivered. Many of the veterans didn't want to wait that long, and would buy surplus military jeeps and other vehicles, re-paint them, and personalize them for their own use.

Some of the women who had joined the work force during the war effort decided that they wanted to stay in the work force. They liked it, and they liked the extra money. Some of them returned home and once again became stay-at-home moms.

There was a major action taken by the government during this period that shaped the future of this country. That was the authorization of what would be called the GI Bill. Under this bill, all service people were offered a free higher education, either at a college or a technical school. Many young people who had never dreamed of, or could afford, a higher education now had the opportunity to get one free of charge, and many, many of them took advantage of it.

* * * * *

In September, Dodo and 122 of her classmates began their senior year at Dickson High. They had the traditional senior activities. Their prom was held in February. In May, they performed a three-act comedy entitled *Star Crazy*, and again, Dodo was the prompter. Her class, and, for that matter, the rest of the school, were enjoying the benefits of the post war transition. The senior annual trip to Washington, D.C. was restored, along with the annual junior class visit to West Point and High Point, New York, and the sophomore educational trip to Hershey and the state capital in Harrisburg.

The athletic program was also affected. Football was reinstated and, as expected, in the first-year program, the team struggled through a one win, five loss season. The baseball team was affected in that the former head coach returned from military service, and resumed his coaching duties. The team responded by finishing second in the league.

The most notable change in this transition was that there were no classmates who had to leave, or who wanted to leave, before graduation to enter the service. Finally, they dedicated both their yearbook, and the graduation ceremony, to the retiring superintendent of the school.

* * * * *

In September of that same year, I enrolled with a full scholarship at the University of Scranton. The school was run by Jesuits, and it was located on Wyoming Avenue in downtown Scranton. It was roughly a 25-minute commute from Dickson by public transportation. Day students were all male. It had no campus or dormitories or any athletic facilities. It did have some fraternities, but there were no fraternity houses. Most of the students were day commuters from various areas of northeastern Pennsylvania. A fair number of students lived outside the commuting area, and they found residence in various private homes in the area.

The student enrollment really swelled, both at the freshman and upper class levels. Many veterans were starting college, while other veterans were returning to complete their college careers that had been interrupted by the war. The ages in our class included 17-year-olds to student in their late 20's and older. In fact, our class president, a fellow Dicksonion, was referred to as Pops because he was probably one of the oldest in the class and had gray hair. This age difference, and the war experiences of the older students, had an interesting side effect in the classrooms. It was not unusual to have a 17- or 18-year-old sitting alongside a 23- or 24-year-old freshman classmate. In fact, it was fairly common.

There were several dozen other Dickson residents who were attending the university at the same time, but I didn't know many of them because of the age difference.

Our philosophy class turned out to be very interesting. Our Jesuit instructor stressed the fact that he was going to teach us how to live rather than how to make a living. His philosophy was that if you lived the proper life, making a living would take care of itself. This theory was reasonably accepted by the teenage students in the class. With the veterans in the class, however, it opened up a whole new area of discussion. After encouragement from the instructor, the veterans offered a description of the real life experiences that they had gone through during the war. They did whatever they had to, to survive to another day. They saw their comrades killed in front of their eyes, and they saw peasants from the various war-torn villages and cities beg for food or offer romantic dalliances with their young women in exchange for food, candy, cigarettes, and nylons. There was quite a gap between ideology and real life.

* * * * *

The age difference also had quite an impact on the various sports. You now had 17- and 18-year-old freshmen, recent all-stars at the high school level, competing for varsity positions against 22- and 23-year-old freshmen, also local high school all-stars but of a prior era.

In early December, basketball tryouts were held under the direction of our head coach, Pete Carlisimo, who had just completed his head football coaching duties. Pete, as well as all of the candidates, was well-versed in basketball fundamentals. Coach informed us that he would make his decisions for positions on the varsity based upon our individual conditioning, aggressiveness, and desire to play the game. After being a starter on the JV team for two weeks, and despite my lack of high school all-star talent or credentials, the coach promoted me to the varsity, primarily due to my display of the characteristics that he had stressed. I would be a member of the varsity basketball team for the rest of my college career.

Without a gymnasium of our own, we resorted to using the facilities at the South Scranton Junior High School. Our practices were held every evening, and we would play our home games there in front of large crowds. In my sophomore year, and for the rest of my career, our basketball activities were transferred to the National Guard Armory in Scranton.

We were a Division 3 school, and most of our games were played against that level, usually against colleges within the state of Pennsylvania. They were normally one-day trips. About a third of our games were played against Division One schools, located up and down the northeastern coast. We would play in cities like New York, Philadelphia, Baltimore, Washington, Buffalo, Olean, and Niagara Falls in northwestern New York. The latter three were usually combined into one extended trip that would last up to 5 or 6 days. We played Division 1 schools like Manhattan Seton Hall, Villanova, LaSalle, George Washington University, St. Bonaventure, Canisus, and Niagara.

We would travel by bus or train depending on our destination. We would carry our own personal luggage, our equipment, and our school assignments, that we were expected to study and keep up with. We spent many hours traveling, and we would spend the time by playing cards, playing Pinochle, or doing our necessary studying.

We played in various large arenas, including Convention Hall in Philadelphia and the Memorial Auditorium in Buffalo, where we played in front of a crowd in excess of 8,000 people. The opportunity and experience participating in the basketball program at the university was really rewarding. I came from my roots at St. Mary's and in the basement gymnasium at Dickson High that seated about a hundred fans and ended up playing in the Memorial Auditorium in Buffalo that seated over 10,000.

* * * * *

During this year, Dodo was very busy with her senior year activities, and socializing with her friends and classmates. I was busy with first-year college activities, especially during the basketball season, when my evenings and most of the weekends were taken up with practice or games, including the travel that we frequently did. My opportunities for social activities really diminished. Dodo and I would run into one another at a high school game, or up at the Towers Recreation Center, but these opportunities were less frequent than they had been in the past. We were still good old friends, though.

In September of 1946, Dodo enrolled in a two-year business program at the Lackawanna Business College in downtown Scranton. I started my sophomore year at the university, and there were some major changes that were taking place. The university had purchased land about 6 or 7 blocks from the original main campus and erected army barracks style buildings to house classrooms that were now needed for the greater influx of students. During the week, it was common to see students hurrying from one campus to the other past the courthouse square in town during their 10-minute break to get from class to class.

Dodo's college was located midway between the two campuses. Several times a week, at the end of our daily class activities, Dodo and I occasionally would end up taking the same bus together back to Dickson. It was only a short bus ride home. (We would sit together, and we would talk.) For the first time, we had an opportunity to spend some time together in a one-on-one situation. We talked about our friends and our families and the activities of both. We talked about our own activities, our outlook on life in general, and our dreams and plans for the future. We learned that neither one of us was dating anybody at the time. During the sharing of our views, our personalities, sense of humor, and underlying sense of silliness surfaced, and we began to realize that we were very compatible. I found myself becoming very attracted to her.

* * * * *

In early November, on one of our short bus rides, I mentioned to Dodo that the university was sponsoring a semi-formal snowball dance over the Christmas holidays. I asked her if she would like to go with me, and in her own casual way she said, "Sure." On December 26, 1946, Dodo and I had our first formal date. I bought her a white gardenia corsage to match the theme of the dance. As I entered the house, there she stood, a real beauty, wearing a beautiful pink gown. We departed her home through the bar so her father could see us. He smiled and said, "Have fun," above the whistles and the "Wows" of the patrons who lined the bar. We stopped at my house so Mom could see how we looked. Mom just raved over Dodo's appearance and the gown she was wearing. Mom saw us off at the door, told me not to step on her feet and have fun. She had a smile on her lips and what looked like a tear in her eye.

We joined my friends and classmates and their dates at the ballroom at the Hotel Jermin. We had fun socializing and dancing to the music of the big bands. At one point, when we were out on the floor dancing, Dodo astonishingly pulled me really close and whispered in my ear, "Dance me slowly with baby steps to the door of the ladies' room." I said, "What?" and she repeated it. I said, "If you have to go to the ladies' room, why can't we just walk over with normal steps?" She said, "Please, the elastic waistband on my half-slip has just snapped; the slip is down around my knees, and I'm afraid if we take normal steps, it'll be on the floor and I'll fall over it and fall on my face." I said, "That's a good reason," and we danced in baby steps all the way to the ladies' room, both of us laughing and enjoying the moment and drawing attention from our friends. As I stood outside the door, waiting and laughing, I said to myself, "This is my kind of girl." In a few minutes she emerged with a silly grin on her face, like nothing had happened. Somewhere she had found a safety pin and made the proper mends. We laughed and danced the rest of the night away.

After the dance, I took her home, and her dad was still awake. We walked in, still laughing, and he said, "There is no need to ask you two if you had fun tonight." When I got home, Mom was still waiting up to hear firsthand how the night had gone. When I told her about the fun we had, she just roared.

We followed up that date with a date on New Year's Eve with our friends. Thereafter, Dodo accompanied me to our games, and we would go out afterwards. On Valentine's Day, we had concluded that we were ready and happy to start a steady and serious relationship. As the months unfolded, we went out on dates, mostly in the company of our friends, who were also dating, including Paul and Ann and Joe and Char and Evelyn and Chas. We would go bowling, dancing, swimming, hiking, or picnicking, depending on what the season permitted.

The next few years seemed to fly by. Our relationship was growing, as well as our compatibility. We shared a fondness for outdoor activities, and our senses of humor complemented each other's'. We started to meet the immediate and extended members of one another's families. We were not only accepted freely by them, but also many of them went beyond that and made us feel like we were actual members of the family.

I took Dodo one day to meet my grandparents, who still only spoke broken English. Grandpa Bart was a man of short stature, very quiet, except for when he had consumed a few adult drinks. Grandma was a fairly tall, stout, jolly woman.

She engulfed Dodo in a warm hug and said, "Bardzo wadha pientka dziewchyna." I told Dodo that she had just said, "You're a very nice, pretty girl." Dodo asked, "How can I thank her?" I told her, and Dodo said, "Dzienkuje, babcia" ("Thank you, Grandma"), as she returned the hug. Grandma then added, "But she's very thin; you'll have to feed her well and fatten her up." Grandpa's only comments were nods and grunts as he rocked in his rocker and expelled tobacco juice into a spittoon.

Grandma's philosophy was that the bigger you were, the healthier you were. She was a perfect poster woman for that philosophy.

Over a twenty-three year period, Grandma was pregnant fifteen times, and five of those pregnancies were multiple conceptions. In fact, during one thirty-month period, she conceived two sets of twins and a set of triplets, but only one each of these multiple conceptions survived beyond birth. WOW. No wonder Grandpa now only had the strength to nod and grunt, and rock and spit.

Dodo took me to meet her lone surviving grandparent, Grandma Lewis, previously known as Lojeski. She was a very short, wiry, and energetic woman. She had owned and worked the farm where Dodo had spent some of her summers. She spoke fluent English, and I don't recall ever hearing her speak Polish.

We immediately hit it off. We were interested in her background, and she enjoyed sharing it. She told us about her experiences growing up as a young girl on a farm in a part of Poland, under German control, near the Black Forest area. We frequently visited Grandma, and at each visit, there were stories, all of them very interesting.

* * * * *

When Dodo got her associate business degree, she and her friend Evelyn decided that Dodo would put this new education to use. They opened up a women's lingerie shop in Dickson, and they called it The Charm Shop. Chas and I painted the walls, made and erected shelves, and loaded the shelves with boxes of stock. The stock was sorted by model, style, and size. The girls didn't have that much seed money with which to start the business, so only the top two or three boxes on each stack had merchandise in them. The rest were there strictly as a display to give the impression that the shop was well stocked. They did a fair amount of business, but after about a year they decided that the shop did not present the financial rewards that they had hoped for, and they closed it.

* * * * *

In 1948, Dodo's brother Teddy died of a heart attack at the age of 29. Teddy had served in the Pacific theater during the war as a member of a bomber crew and had participated in over 25 missions. There seemed to be a special bond between Dodo and her brother, and she was devastated when he died. He was her older brother, and he had looked after her. He loved to tease her, make her laugh, and, at times, he provoked her just to get some reaction. She loved it. She found it difficult to say no to any of his requests. There were times when we were planning to go out for the evening, and at the last minute he would come in and plead with her to babysit his infant daughter, Terry, so he could take his wife, Eleanor, out on the town. Dodo would play hard to get, just to see and hear his facial and verbal contortions as he pleaded his case. In the end, we would babysit. It took Dodo a while to get over the emotional shock of his death, but over time she did.

* * * * *

In my junior year of college, I was picked as a starter on the varsity basketball team, and in my senior year, I was elected co-caption. Dodo became a fixture at our games. She was occasionally joined by friends of ours or by my Uncle Iggy; his wife, Ann, and their son, Jerry. She was most often joined by my mother; father; sister Lorraine, and brother Gene. My mother always insisted on sitting with Dodo at the games, and so did Lorraine and Gene. My mother said that Dodo could calm her down during the exciting parts of the game. They would banish Dad to the other side of the court, where he could vent his occasionally out-of-control emotions.

During the periods of non-game action, like pre game or half time, or even post game when they were waiting for me to come out of the locker room, Dodo and Mom were in relatively constant conversation. It was becoming apparent that there was a closeness developing there that would match any deep mother/daughter relationship.

CHAPTER TWELVE
STARTING LIFE TOGETHER

In June of 1949, I received my Bachelor of Science degree with a major in social studies and a temporary teaching certificate from the University of Scranton. Teaching positions were not readily available at the time. Many veterans had come back from the war and reclaimed their previous teaching jobs, and the baby boom generation was just in its infancy. I applied for a couple of jobs out in the country, and when I would go for an interview, Dodo would accompany me. We would scout out the town to see if it was the type of town that we would like to settle in. My interviews went favorably, but I was facing the effects of the war. My competitors were veterans, older in age, who had served their time in the service, while I was still young, 20 years old and 1A in the draft. I was unsuccessful in getting a teaching position.

In the spring of 1950, Dodo and I, now 21, were working full time for nominal wages and trying to save some money for our future marriage. Friends of ours encouraged us to accompany them to work for the summer at resort hotels in the Catskill Mountains in New York. They had worked there the previous summer or two, and told us that you could make more money in a week up there than you could in a month back in town. They offered to help us get jobs at their respective hotels. Dodo and I agreed that we would go and work there for the summer. The jobs proved more rewarding than even we had anticipated. We got jobs at adjoining hotels. She was hired as a chamber maid and I as a waiter in a children's dining room. We worked 7 days a week. We had a salary of $40 a month, plus free room and board, plus tips. The tips made the big difference.

As we were settling into our new jobs and new environment, President Truman announced that he was sending army troops to South Korea to help that country protect their freedom and to stop the influx of Communism from the north. We were concerned with this new national development, but the President said that it was only a police action.

Along about mid-summer, Dodo and I were starting to discuss what we would do, and what our future plans would be, when our summer employment ended around the middle of September. We discussed the pros and cons of various options. One night during one of these discussions, I looked over and I said, "Dodo, why don't we just get married and start our life together?" She looked at me, and said, "That sounds like a good idea, why not?" That was how I proposed to her, and that was how she accepted it.

We agreed that we would get married on the first Saturday in October. We also agreed that, under the circumstances, we would have a morning ceremony followed by a brunch reception for our immediate families that would include our siblings, parents, and grandparents. We were granted a day off from work, and we came home to notify our parents and make the necessary religious and social arrangements.

Our parents were happy for us, particularly Mom. As she warmly hugged us with a big smile on her face and tear-laden eyes, she proceeded to tell us a story. When Dodo and I were infants, my mother and Bella Buza would take us for walks in our carriages. They would frequently meet and join up in their walks. During one of those walks, Bella peeked into my carriage and said, "Mary, that's a cute son you have there; I would sure like to adopt him as my own." My mother peeked into Dodo's carriage and said, "That's a cute daughter you have there Bella; I sure would like to adopt her as my own." Bella laughed and said, "Wouldn't it be nice if one day they grew up and got married? That way, each one of us could share them both." My mother then said, "Now I'll have that pleasure."

We met with our pastor, Father Dominiak, the one whom I had led into church at his installation as pastor some 7 years earlier. He greeted us warmly and was happy when he found out the purpose of our visit. He laughed when he was looking up our parish records at the coincidence that our last names both started with "B," that we had been born in the same year and month, and that we were baptized in the same month. He happily agreed to perform our ceremony.

We returned from the mountains in September and were quite busy following through on all the necessary arrangements. In addition, we sought and found employment. We signed a 3-month lease on a two-room furnished apartment in Scranton, and I notified the draft board, requesting that they change my status from single to married. They responded with a letter, informing me that I was to report for a physical on the 11th of October.

* * * * *

October 7, 1950, dawned as a picture perfect fall day. The church was beautifully decorated with appropriate fall flower arrangements. My good friend Charlie was my best man, and Dodo's sister Evelyn was her maid of honor. Although our reception was limited to immediate family members, our extended families turned out in full force to witness our ceremony, congratulate us, and wish us well. For the first time in Dodo's adult life, she took center stage at the ceremony. She walked down the aisle on the arm of her father, in her own shy, demure way, looking radiantly beautiful in a gorgeous white satin and lace gown.

Our reception was held at the upper level dining area of Johnny Hot Dog's Tavern (Town House) on Main Street in Dickson. Everything went as planned, and we were cheered by our friends and acquaintances who were seated at the lower level bar. Later that afternoon, we drove up to the Strickland's Inn in the Pocono Mountains for our honeymoon. There we joined other young newlyweds in a couple days of fun activities that were planned by the hotel.

Upon our return, I took my physical and passed. We settled in to our two-room apartment. Dodo was not an experienced cook, but she had learned the basics by observing and helping her sister Ceil and Bell as they prepared the meals while she was growing up. Dodo decided that every night she would try something new for dinner. At the end of each meal, she would ask me for my comments and ask how it was. I'd say it was great, because it was. After about a week or two of this routine, one night she said to me, "I'd really like your honest opinion, because if there is anything I should change, I'd like to know."

I said, "No, Dodo, everything is great the way you are fixing it."

She said, "Well, I'm getting the feeling that you'd say that just to be nice, and even if I served you dirt, you would say it was great." I said, "No, no, no Dod, uh uh."

A couple nights later, I came home and walked into the great aroma in the kitchen. We were preparing to sit down to dinner, and she took a small dish out of the oven and nonchalantly placed it in front of me. I noticed that it was dirt. I took a couple grains of the dirt and put it in my mouth, pretended I was chewing and said, "Dodo, this is great."

She said, "What are you doing? That's dirt!"

I said, "It tastes great to me."

She said, "I knew it; I said you would say everything I prepared was great. You're crazy!"

And I said, "Yes, aren't we both."

Before we knew it, it was Christmas Eve and Dodo's twenty-second birthday. Her sister Evelyn and our friend Johnny came down and joined us for some cake and ice cream and to sing Happy Birthday. We realized that we didn't have a Christmas tree, and we needed one for our first Christmas together. The girls sent us men out to find a tree, a foot or two tall, that we could place on a night stand next to our bed. We were unable to find a tree that size, and we ended up buying a tree that was about 5 feet tall and not quite as wide. As we came through the door with the tree, Dodo said, "What the heck are you doing with that; where are we going to put it?" We moved the night table away from the bed and stood the Christmas tree up. Dodo decorated it with tinsel and blue lights.

That night as we were going to bed, she realized that she had to get into the bed from my side, because her side was blocked by the tree. She got in and reclined, and just above her head was a tip of a branch, with several strands of tinsel dangling and shimmering in the light. She lay there and was blowing up at them to make them shimmer even more. We both laughed hysterically. I said, "Happy Birthday, Dodo." And we wished each other a merry Christmas.

As the New Year of 1951 was being rung in, Dodo called her dad to wish him happy New Year, as she traditionally did.

* * * * *

The police action in Korea had now escalated into a war. We were taking casualties, and monthly induction rates were now being increased. We had moved into a new apartment in Scranton overlooking the city. We spent a good amount of that time, besides working, socializing with our friends Paul and Ann and Chas and Evey, who also now were married. We would visit with Paul and Ann on weekends, and we would play canasta or double deck pinochle, and we would just relax and drink and talk. The girls did most of the talking, and then, in fact, they would be so engaged in conversation that Paul and I would test it every once in a while and try to cheat a little bit, but they were always aware of what was happening in the game, and they would catch us.

We occasionally went sightseeing, and to ball games in New York. Occasionally, we would go to Bridgeport, Connecticut, to visit Dodo's sister, Belle, and her husband, Johnny. During our visits to Connecticut, Belle and Johnny would encourage us to move on up to Bridgeport, where better paying jobs were more readily available. At the end of 1951, we moved in temporarily with Belle and Johnny.

CHAPTER THIRTEEN
ARMY SERVICE

We rapidly settled into our new environment in Connecticut. We were able to successfully find good paying jobs. We started to look at apartments, and I sent a letter to the draft board in Scranton, notifying them of a change in address. They responded by ordering me to report for induction to serve a two-year tour of duty in the Army.

On April 15, 1952, Dodo and Mom and Dad saw me off at the train station in Scranton as I departed with a group of other inductees to Fort Mead, Maryland, for processing. After about a week of processing and taking various tests, I was assigned to Camp Gordon, Georgia, for 8 weeks of basic training. The camp was located on the outskirts of Augusta, in a rural, depressed area, and the terrain consisted mostly of sand with a few pine trees and a lot of snakes.

Not quite midway through basic training, on May 18, Dodo's dad died after a prolonged bout with cancer. He was a gentleman in the truest sense of the word, and he was a very successful businessman. His tavern was modest, but it was a first-class operation. He had strict rules in that he didn't allow profoundly loud personal arguments, and, above all, he obeyed the law and refused to serve anybody under the age of 21 an alcoholic drink. In fact, when Dodo and I were dating, and the family would gather over the holidays, he would make sure that we were not served an alcoholic drink and promised us that on our 21st birthday, he would pour us our first drink, and he did. He would serve sandwiches and snacks, and he had a back room with tables where couples could sit and relax or they could come up to the bar where many couples felt comfortable sitting.

Although the state's blue laws prohibited bars from being open on Sundays, they all conducted business by allowing the patrons access by ringing the back door bell. As he opened the back door to allow a patron in, he would ask them if they had been to church and, if they said they had been, he would invite them in and buy them their first drink. But if they had not, he would tell them they still had time to make the next Mass and that they could come back later. During the war years, he never took a penny from a serviceman, and all of their drinks were on him.

Several weeks after her father's death, Dodo took a 25-hour bus trip and came down to visit me for a weekend. Our orders had come through and, following the completion of basic training, I was scheduled to remain at the camp and attend a 24-week course in field radio operation and repair. This would be followed by a 10-day leave of absence and immediate deployment to Korea. Dodo was looking forward to moving down so that we could spend those 24 weeks together, but during her visit there, we found that affordable off-post housing was minimal or virtually nonexistent. We agreed that I would register for on-post military housing, but we recognized that it might take some time before it would come through.

On the last day of basic training, a Friday, we were packing our belongings in preparation for moving out to a new company location. Around noon, 4 of us were called up to the company headquarters and advised that our orders had been changed. We had an hour to get packed, at which time we would be transported to Augusta aboard the 2 o'clock overnight train to New York. From there, we would be transported to Fort Monmouth, New Jersey, to attend a 24-week training course in fire control. Nobody knew what fire control meant.

At the train station, we met up with a dozen other soldiers whose orders had also been changed at the last minute. On our train ride north, we introduced ourselves, engaged in conversation, and tried to determine what fire control meant, why our orders had been changed at the last minute, and why we were the ones selected. We didn't come up with any answers, but during the conversations, we came up with one common denominator -- we had all attended or graduated from college.

We arrived at Fort Monmouth early Saturday afternoon. We signed in. We were given a temporary bunk area and were issued a 36-hour pass. On the way north, I didn't have the opportunity or access to a phone where I could call Dodo and give her the good news. I was scheduled to call her Saturday afternoon from Georgia and give her my new location and other pertinent data. Now I had the opportunity to either call her or deliver the good news in person, and I chose the latter. I concluded that taking commercial transportation from the camp via New York City back to Scranton and then onto Dickson could easily take me 6 hours or more depending on the various time tables involved, and I felt that I could do better just by hitchhiking home. Hitchhiking by servicemen was a common and acceptable mode of transportation in those days, and people would readily stop to give a serviceman a lift.

I went out on the highway with my home town scribbled on a cardboard sign and quickly got 2 rides and found myself more than halfway home, in Stroudsburg, Pennsylvania. There again I was quickly picked up by 2 young men from New York who were heading to Scranton for a weekend. We got to talking. They asked me my story, and I told them, and they said they were taking me right home. They dropped me off at the Buza home. I thanked them profusely and knocked at the door. Dodo opened the door and, in shock, she said, "I thought you were in Georgia; how did you get here?" along with a dozen other questions. She quickly calmed down as I told her I was there to personally deliver the good news to my best friend, which she always claimed she was, and she was right.

We were really overjoyed with the change in direction that my Army career was taking. Back at Fort Monmouth on Monday, my colleagues and I were transferred to Camp Wood, which was an annex of Fort Monmouth. We were assigned to 2 8-men squad tents that had wooden floors and roll-up side flaps. It was summer, so it was just like an extended camping trip. We were called in to a cinder block building which would be the site of our future classroom, and we were given a briefing.

We were told that we had been selected as candidates for this new fire control course based on the mathematical and analytical capabilities that we had demonstrated through attending college. We were also told that the Army was using the term "fire control" to define hardware and technology used to determine the appropriate position of big guns at appropriate targets.

The course we had been selected for would be conducted in 4 distinct, yet progressive, phases. Our successful absorption of the material being taught in each phase would qualify us to move to the next phase, and all 4 phases combined would take us through 12 months of training. The Army was giving me a fantastic opportunity, and I was determined to make the most of it.

The first phase of our training was a 12-week course in basic electronics. There we learned the design and function and purpose of vacuum tubes, resistors, transformers, and capacitors, and we learned the difference between series and parallel circuits. The need for a mathematical background became evident as we had to learn and apply numerous formulas in the field of electronics. We spent a fair amount of our free time in studying. This was a field that I had never considered while in college. I found it somewhat challenging, but very interesting. Eventually, it became very enjoyable, and I qualified for the next phase.

The next 12-week phase, we learned about the theory and operational characteristics of basic radar and analog computer systems. We also learned how the hardware that we had previously studied was combined to form a functioning system. We did a lot more free time studying, as now our mathematical and analytical capabilities were being expanded. The extra studying paid off, and I successfully passed this phase of the training.

After a short furlough over the Christmas holidays, we reported to the Aberdeen proving ground in Maryland outside the town of the same name. It was located some 25 minutes north of Baltimore. Here again we were the lead group that was coming through a new, highly technical Army training course. We were detached from the normal student companies. In fact, we were assigned to a permanent company for billeting, and we were not required to perform KP or guard duty or other Army housekeeping duties.

Our 24-week training program at Aberdeen was divided into two 12-week phases. In each phase, we learned the operational theory of each system and got actual hands-on experience. We became proficient in operating, maintaining, and repairing both systems. Both systems were in their initial production phases and would shortly begin being deployed within the United States.

In order to accommodate the extensive hands-on training that would be required on a limited number of prototype systems that were available to the school, the course was run on a double shift basis. I was assigned to the group that would attend daily classes from 3 p.m. until 11 p.m. In the first 12-week phase, we concentrated on the larger of the two fire control systems. Our instructors were mostly military personal with a rank no higher than a corporal. Most, if not all, had attended and graduated college. They had gone through a training course sponsored by the production contractor, and they used that data then to develop the program of instruction for the Army. They were joined by a cadre of contractor tech reps in teaching the course.

Our first few weeks were spent in the classroom, where we studied the performance characteristics of the major components of the system and how they were integrated and interconnected to produce and enhance the system's capabilities.

We were also introduced to what was known and described as the heart of the relay system, the magnetron. This item was about a cubic foot in size and consisted of stacks of horseshoe-sized magnets arranged around an inner circle of tubes and cavities. When energized, the magnetron would generate a powerful microwave signal that was transmitted into space and used to detect and track targets.

We were cautioned that whenever we were working a magnetron in its static or unpowered state, we needed to make sure that we had no metallic objects in close proximity like dog tags or screwdrivers or other tools, because they would be sucked into this magnetic field and attached to the magnets in such a way that it would be hard to dislodge them. The cabinet doors that secured the magnetron in its cabinet had to be closed and locked before the unit could be fired up. Again we were cautioned to make sure that no tools or other metallic objects were in proximity to the magnetron before we closed the doors, because once it was fired up, these items would not only be attached to the magnets, but they would also melt in a matter of seconds from the power being generated.

With typical Army ingenuity, we soon learned that we could heat up food or liquids in a matter of seconds in non-metallic containers. Typically on a Friday night as the school week was coming to an end and we were ready to hit the road and depart for our various weekend destinations, we would heat up some food in a little liquid to serve as a snack before we departed. Ironically, it was this type of item that gave birth to the development and production of our common kitchen microwave ovens.

Next, we moved on to the hands-on phase of the training. Except for two rear antennae, all of the rest of the components that made up the system were lined up, attached to the walls of what was essentially a semi-trailer-sized van. The tracking radar dish was mounted on the roof of the van, while the acquisition radar dish was detached about 30 feet away. Also situated in the van was a 7-foot-wide operator's control console. There were 3 stations, and each one had a display screen along with associated manual controls. Each station was designed to track a certain data point to the target. One tracked the asmit. Another tracked the target's altitude, and the third tracked the range of the target. When a target was detected by the acquisition radar during its continual 360 degree sweep, it would appear as a bleep on each of the operator's screens. Each of the operators would then manually maneuver their marker and superimpose it right onto the target. In so doing, they were positioning the rooftop mounted tracking radar to a position pointed right at the target. After maintaining coincidence between their marker and the target for several seconds, the operators would switch over to automatic control, and the system would take over automatic tracking of the target. The generated tracking data was continually being fed into the computer. This data, along with other variables such as the time of flight required for the shell to reach the target, would be computed, and a firing solution would be determined.

These solutions were furnished to the gun sites that were pin wheeled around the radar site, and the guns would be fired at the appropriate setting so that the 90-millimeter shell would intersect the target.

As part of our training, we had to become proficient in operating the system, particularly at the 3 tracking stations. As we did, the instructors started to introduce malfunctions into the system or to actually disable certain segments of it. We worked as a 3-man team, and we operated the system and detected and analyzed any problem and then corrected the problem by replacing the defective parts that the instructors had inserted into the system.

This type of troubleshooting exercise actually made up a major portion of our final exam. We all passed. The instructors were happy that they had done a good job of presenting the material. We felt happy that we were able to absorb it all.

The final 12 weeks of our training program were essentially a duplicate of the previous phase. We studied the smaller of the 2 systems that included similar technology and theory. The system was much more compact and mobile. It was designed to bring down targets at lower altitudes and closer ranges. It was equally effective while being operated in either the automatic or manual tracking mode. All of the system components, including the associated 75 millimeter gun and a dozen rounds of ammo, were contained on a rotating platform. The radar compartment and the loan radar operator were located on one side of the gun tube, while the computer compartment and its operator were located on the other side. The gun crew was stationed at the back of the platform. During operation, the entire system and crew were exposed to weather elements. During extreme cold, the crew would be operating with partially numb fingers or wearing heavy winter gloves that would diminish their dexterity.

The radar operator at his post had a screen and several controls. On top of his cabinet was mounted an antenna with a 30-inch diameter. This antenna could be used to scan a 360-degree rotation, or it could be used to track and lock onto a target. When the operator locked onto a target, the system would rotate, and the gun would elevate to an appropriate target lead position.

The electromechanical computer operator had his own manual controls, and he had a periscope with which he could visually eyeball the target. When in the manual tracking mode, he was the one who would control the position of the system.

The system had quite a technical concept and circuit designed into it called a secant potentiamotor or, as we used to call it, a pot. The circuit came into play on targets that were coming in and would pass directly over the system. With the system in auto tracking mode, and the gun reaching maximum elevations, this circuit output data would rotate the system 180 degrees to allow the system to continue tracking as the target moved away. The technique to determine if the system was operating correctly in this mode was quite involved and extensive. However, with typical Army ingenuity, we found a way to test the system faster and better.

Located near us on the base was a landing strip where small Army aircraft frequently came in for a landing. Their path would take them directly over our site, at just several hundred feet of altitude. We would lock onto one of these targets to verify that our system was tracking. This tracking technique was very effective, but after about a month, our commander got a call from the airport commander telling us to knock it off. It seems that his pilots were getting very nervous when they were coming in on their flight path and found themselves looking down the tube of a 75-millimeter gun that was tracking them.

* * * * *

Before we knew it, we had graduated the fire control school at Aberdeen, roughly one year after we had started at Fort Monmouth. We were then assigned to an organization that was called the Unit Training Center. This center was headed up by a chief warrant officer who had several instructors and several fire control systems at his disposal. The graduates were assigned to and made up the bulk of a 6-man fire control repair team that was now headed up by a warrant officer. They would use a number of military vehicles, including a truck that contained all of their test equipment and another truck that acted as their repair shop.

They trained as a team for a few weeks and would actually respond to service calls from the center. The center instructors watched them and saw how they went through the analysis and the repair and would grade and approve their performance. The team was then deployed to a major city around the perimeter of the United States. They were deployed mostly to the East or West Coasts to maintain and repair the fire control systems that were being installed at those locations.

When I reported to the Unit Training Center, the chief warrant officer, a fellow by the name of Ernie Inman, a down-to-earth Midwesterner who had monitored our progress through the school and who, in fact, had instructed several classes for us, asked me if I preferred to be assigned to one of the teams that was to ship out or whether I would like to stay on as an instructor for him at Aberdeen for the remaining 9 to 10 months of my tour of duty. I discussed this with Dodo, and we both agreed and were happy to stay on at Aberdeen.

* * * * *

During the last 4 months of my training at Fort Monmouth, Dodo was able to join me. We joined with 3 of my classmates who had also gone through basic training with me and their wives who were now also joining them. We rented a large, furnished home about a block or two off the beach in Asbury Park, New Jersey. It had 4 bedrooms, two kitchens on different levels, and adequate bathroom facilities. It was located in close proximity to the church, stores, and public transportation and was only about a 10-minute ride to the base. We shared a kitchen with Hollis and Anna Fey, a wonderful young couple from Nanchdosis, Texas. The other kitchen was shared by Walter and Jenntta and Paul and Henretta and both couples were from Campbellsville, Kentucky.

All three couples had that Southern charm and manners and were very respectful and more so to us because we were the oldest couple by about 6 months. In fact, they were uncomfortable calling Dodo by the name Dodo, and they soon switched to calling her Ms. Doddy.

We spent a lot of time on weekends in joint activities. Primarily we would do sightseeing. We would ride the train into New York City to see the various sites, or we would go up and down the northern New Jersey coast and take in the coastal sites. And, of course, I and Ms. Doddy, as the Northerners, were the tour guides. One Saturday a month, we would host a dinner party. One couple would prepare the appetizers; another couple would provide the liquid refreshments; another couple would prepare the desserts, and the fourth couple would prepare a dinner that was traditional in their part of the country. We were introduced to and really enjoyed their Southern cooking and the customs and traditions that went with it

We would also host the Halloween party. Everybody would make up their homemade costumes. They performed skits as couples either reflecting their costume theme or something native to their area of the country, and we would play games and even bob for apples. We were just all young kids again.

As I was preparing to transition to the Aberdeen proving ground, we spent the Christmas furlough holidays with Belle and Johnny. They suggested, and we agreed, that Dodo should stay with them until I could get us settled at Aberdeen. When I reported to Aberdeen, and found that I would be having classes from 3 to 11 p.m. daily and having weekends free, Belle and Johnny recommended that Dodo stay with them during the duration of my training, where she could get a financially rewarding job and I could commute on weekends to Connecticut. We agreed.

Belle and Johnny, who was a submariner in WWII, not only opened their home to us, but they also really went out of their way to make us feel like it was our home too. They were a real pillar of support to us. They looked out for us, and they really tried to help us. We never forgot it. In fact, Johnny really went out of his way and searched to find me a used car with low mileage that had been well maintained. He succeeded, and as a result, I had the wheels to commute every weekend. They showed us the true meaning of family love and support.

As my formal training was coming to an end and I found out that I would be staying at Aberdeen for the remainder of my tour of duty, Dodo joined me. We found an apartment in a military housing complex at Edgewood, Maryland, midway between Baltimore and Aberdeen. It was probably a 20-minute commute to each destination.

The train station was within 2 blocks of our apartment, and Dodo found and commuted to a job in Baltimore. As with her previous jobs, she was working in the business office of a company where she worked on payroll and other business-related activities. She was good in the business field, and we both came from the old school where we always felt that no matter what job you held, you did your best.

I guess I did mine well enough, for at one point I was selected to and did receive the battalion soldier of the month award.

There was an old saying at that time that no matter where you went sooner or later you would run into someone from Dickson City. One day, while Dodo and I were shopping at the PX on the Post, sure enough we ran into my cousin Jerry Bart. We knew he was in the Army, but we had no idea he was stationed at the same post.

Dodo's oldest sister, Toni, was a public health service officer, and she was stationed in a military hospital in the Washington area and living in a nearby community. We would occasionally join her for dinner on the weekends.

As my discharge date was coming up, one of the contractor representatives who were stationed with us offered me a job as a contractor tech rep for his company. The job required occasional moving and quite a bit of traveling, so I graciously declined. Around the same time, my boss, Warrant Officer Ernie, Mr. Ernie as we called him, asked me if I was interested in working for the Army as a civilian civil service employee at the Frankford Arsenal in northeast Philadelphia in my home state of Pennsylvania.

The Frankford Arsenal was an Army installation headed up by an Army officer with the rank of colonel. The workforce consisted mostly of civilians, as did their management structure. This installation was the Army agency responsible for the production and deployment of the two radar systems that I had been training on. They had a maintenance job there that was responsible for maintaining liaison with the troops in the field who were using, operating, and maintaining these systems. That organization was now beginning to train their employees on the operation and maintenance of just one of those systems. Ernie thought I would be a perfect fit for that group.

Dodo and I discussed it, and we concluded that it would be a perfect opportunity for us. Ernie took me along on his next liaison visit to the Arsenal, and he had prearranged for me to be introduced and interviewed by the appropriate people. He was right. They offered me a package, and I accepted it. It was much better with better benefits than even Dodo and I had anticipated, and they were anxious for me to get started working for them as soon after my discharge as the processing of the paperwork would permit.

Dodo and I were really happy with this new development, as were her sister Ceil and her husband, Charlie. They were living in Levittown, Pennsylvania, which was a new town where the home construction was really just getting started. It was only 30 minutes northeast of the Arsenal, and they were really happy that we would be moving into their area. They offered us all the relocation help we would need.

On April 15, 1954, I received an honorable discharge from the Army. We were one young, happy couple that day as we drove north, knowing that my tour of duty in the Army was over. We reminisced about the previous 24 months and that day when I was inducted and didn't know where the Army was going to send me, or what they were going to have me do. And that fateful last day of basic training when the Army changed my orders from a path that would in all probabilities have taken me to Korea and selected me to go through an expensive, extensive, technical training program in a new technological field. Now, because of that training, I was heading into a promising career with long-term job possibilities.

Dodo, in her own inimitable way, said, "You know, it's funny; the Army didn't waste their money or your time giving you that training because ironically now you are going to go back to work for them and give them back the benefits of that training. Thank you, Army."

CHAPTER FOURTEEN

JOBS

On the way north to my new career field, I got to reminiscing about the various jobs I had held. None of these jobs gave me the slightest inkling of what my career would be.

While in high school, I had tried to establish an impressive resume. I had worked part-time before or after school hours, full-time in the summer, and didn't hesitate to switch to a different job that offered perks or higher wages. By the time I graduated from high school, I had a diversified resume.

Following my freshman year in the early summer of 1942, I was hired for a day job fixing the weekly accumulation of flat tires experienced by a dry cleaning company's fleet of minivan, pick-up and delivery trucks. Flats were a common occurrence during the war years, because everybody was riding around on recap tires due to the rationing and scarcity of new tires. I knew how to locate the tire tube leak, hot patch and test it, and remount and inflate the tire. The shop foreman informed me that their tire gauge was very unreliable and that while inflating I should also press on the sidewall to confirm the adequacy of the pressure. After an hour or so, the foreman came over to check on my progress. He was pleased with the repairs I had done and later did in another hour or so.

Later, as I was pressing on the sidewall of a nearly fully inflated tire, it blew with a loud bang and scared the hell out of me. The foreman came running over and gave out a big sigh of relief when he saw me standing, shaken, but unhurt. At that point he said, "I like you, kid, so I'm paying you a day's wages and, out of concern for your safety, I'm sending you home."

* * * * *

A few weeks later, in early July, I was dispatched to Pittsburgh for the rest of the summer to live with my godmother, Aunt Gen, and her family, and to work as a stock boy in a Kroger grocery store that her husband Walter managed. The time period coincided with the last several weeks of Mom's pregnancy and, on August 2, Mom gave birth to my baby brother Ronald. A couple of weeks later, I returned home with my earnings and a number of cans of vegetables, whose labels had fallen off and thus weren't sellable. Thereafter, we had some fun as we guessed what veggies we were to have for supper before opening the can.

* * * * *

For the next year or so, I worked at our local dairy helping the owner deliver milk to residential and commercial customers. We would begin our home delivery run by 5:30 a.m. and complete it by 8 a.m., even on Fridays when we delivered orders for farmer's cheese that women used to make pierogis. On school days, I would reload the truck for his commercial run and hustle home to get ready for school. On Saturdays, and throughout the summer, I would accompany him on both runs and afterwards assist in steam cleaning the shop and pasteurizing equipment. Since we used an open bed truck, we would cover the milk with a heavy tarp to keep it from freezing. In the summer, we would place chunks of ice under the tarp to keep the milk cool. Perks of this job included being able to drink whatever milk I wanted, and I loved chocolate milk.

* * * * *

In my junior year, I tired of waking so early six days a week and accepted a job as one of about 4 ushers in our town theater, called the Rex. We had two nightly 2-hour showings beginning at 7 p.m.; a feature Sunday matinee and a slightly more than 4 -hour Saturday afternoon children's matinee. The evening showings were usually routine and uneventful, even for the most popular hit movies when the theater would be filled to capacity. We used these evenings to meet, chat, and later socialize with unattached young and some older female peers, including ones from lower Throop, as well as with Dodo and Frank. On the other hand, the Saturday children's matinee was pure bedlam. All afternoon, the theater was filled with the sounds of oohs and cheers, and boos, and screams of laughter, joy, or fear as the youngsters reacted to the various scenes.

Well before the matinee started, the theater would rapidly fill with kids. By show time, every one of the approximately 1,000 seats would be occupied. On many seats, 2 kids would sit together. The program would consist of a showing of a newsreel, a cartoon(s) an "A" feature film and a "B" western wherein the hero wore a white hat and rode a smart horse that could do tricks. The bad guy wore a black hat, and occasionally they would fire as many as ten shots from their six shooter without reloading.

Also shown sequentially every week was one of twelve ten-minute Chapters that featured a hero and his girlfriend fighting the bad guys. Every segment ended with the kids screaming in fear as our hero or his girlfriend found themselves in a sure death situation. Many kids could be overheard contemplating an escape plan. The next week, they would cheer as an obviously simple escape was accomplished, only to scream again at the end.

The highlight of the matinee came at the end when we ran a ten-minute film of one of ten different races (automobile, horseback, bicycle, foot, etc.). The same elderly stumbling keystone cop type characters competed in each race, and each was in the lead at some point in each race. As the kids, including my siblings, Lorraine (9) and Gene (7) entered the theater, they were each given a ticket numbered 1 to 10. The child holding the winning race ticket would receive a large Hershey chocolate candy bar on the way out. On any given Saturday, I knew the winning ticket number and race to be shown and would make sure that, unbeknownst to them, one of my siblings would receive a winning ticket.

Before the race began, the kids would all be cheering. When the race started, it would be pure bedlam as each racer took his turn in the lead. Ten percent of the kids would be on their feet cheering and clapping, and when their racer fell back into the pack, they would fall back into their seats booing, hissing, and completely spent. For some, the excitement was too much, and we would quickly have lines to the restrooms as they shouted, "Hurry up!"

It was fun watching my siblings experience similar energetic reactions. It was even more fun when they realized that they held a winning ticket. By the time they walked a half block, they meticulously halved the candy bar and, in short order, Gene would have devoured his and Lorraine would have let hers melt and linger in her mouth. Mom often remarked that giving them their 25 cents weekly allowance to attend the matinee was money well spent, because they would be safely gone for the afternoon; she had relaxing quiet, and they weren't very hungry when they returned.

* * * * *

One summer, I entered the 40-hour workweek force as I worked at two different garment-producing facilities. The first was where women sewed woolen winter army uniforms. My job was to carry the material to the sewing stations and to collect the finished garments. After a couple of weeks of handling wool in the heat of the summer, and heat generated by the sewing machines, in a loft that had open windows as air conditioning, I switched to a job in a civilian garment-producing factory. I worked as a sales clerk in our outlet sales room, where we sold order overruns and slightly imperfect garments at reduced prices, and I bought clothes at cost.

* * * * *

At the end of the basketball season in my senior year, I joined my classmate and friend "Bozo" in working 3 to 4 hours a day after school at the American Tobacco Company in Scranton where they produced El Rol Tan cigars. Our main job was to create holes in the mouth end to eliminate the need to bite off the tip. We would use a fixture of needles to do ten cigars at a time. I continued at this job on a full-time basis into the summer, and during this time, also learned how to roll a cigar. Every week, I could and did buy a box of cigars for a dollar, and we would give them to Mom's brother Johnny. Dad would also hand them out to select friends.

* * * * *

During my enrollment in college, I confined my work for pay efforts to the summer months. One summer, I worked as a laborer on the surface of a local coal mine. This was where Dad and his brother worked underground and where another brother, Chet, miraculously survived a mine roof cave in. I worked on a crew that was responsible for various tasks around the mine. These tasks included general maintenance of building and mine cars, rails, and loaded mine cars with timbers up to 10 feet in length and other materials required in the mine.

For a 2-week period, I worked as a fill-in at the tipple house, where the mine coal cars were weighed and the coal weight content would be credited to the miner whose numbered metal tag was removed from the side of the car. Since he was paid by the ton, that weight would help determine his next pay amount. Finally, one end of the car would be raised and the coal would be dumped into a pit, where it would fall onto a conveyor belt and be carried to the top of the breaker for processing.

During the 8-hour shift, I was a member of a three-man crew in which one man was responsible for removing the miner's tag from the car. The other two were required to open a latch on both sides of the front end, swing out door. The three of us would rotate positions about every 20 minutes.

Popping the latch open required only stamina and good reflexes. We would stand outside the opposite track rails and, upon a bell signal from the mostly enclosed weighing office that signaled the elevating of the back of the car, we would immediately and simultaneously give the latches a hard hit using about a 3-feet-long steel rod with a flat steel hammer head. Failure to timely pop a latch, which rarely happened, created shouts of obscenities, since the car then had to be lowered to relieve the pressure of the coal on the door and the latch. We worked in a relatively constant coal dust environment that only varied in degree and that was evident at the end of shift, in the coating of dust that covered our clothes and exposed body parts.

At the mine, I met some other young lads, recent high school graduates, a couple of whom were outstanding athletes who lacked the desire or finances to extend their formal education. I realized the bleak and financially modest employment future they and their future families would face.

I saw men ride up the mine slope, seated on the floor of a mine car, their heads bent to avoid overhead timbers as they exited the mine. Their features were indistinguishable, except for the white of their eyes, as they and their clothing were blackened by coal dust. Their work area was safer than in previous decades; nevertheless, roof cave-ins and accidents that resulted in death or disabling injuries still occurred, and as the mine whistles would blare.

In 1927, one month after being in Mom's wedding party, her 20-year-old brother, Louis, was killed in a mine explosion and fire. His father was prevented from getting to his screaming son by a wall of debris between them. Years later, we attended the funeral of Mom's Uncle John, who was killed in a mine cave-in and left a widow and their very young daughter.

I visited Uncle Chet, my godfather, at the hospital when he was recuperating from injuries he received during a roof collapse during which he miraculously escaped death. He was trapped under the debris, and it took extraordinary strength by Dad and his 2 other crew members to move a large chunk of debris and pull Chet to safety.

Dodo's family wasn't spared these experiences, as her aunt's husband, Frank, died at a young age from coal miner's black lung disease, leaving his wife with three young children to raise. Other families had similar experiences. Our neighbor was killed under a roof cave-in, and my friend's father died after being unable to fully recover from a partial leg amputation, the result of a mine accident.

The experience of working at the coal mine and the exposure to the work conditions and risks came at an appropriate time in my life. I was embarking on the pursuit of a college degree and contemplating a future career. It instilled in me a greater incentive to take advantage of my scholarship and earn a degree.

* * * * *

Later in college, I worked at a beer distributing company in Scranton as a delivery helper. Two days per week, we would deliver a couple of hundred cases of Ballentine, Kaiers, and Goebells bottled beer to taverns and restaurants in Center City. Two days per week, we would deliver more draft than bottled beer to outlying community establishments, and I learned how to carefully tap a half of beer. On Wednesdays, I worked the dock area serving drive-in customers or helped unload a freight car full of cases of Ballentines beer and ale. We would take the bottles from the first few cases and place them in a tub filled with ice to quench our thirst. One really hot day, I quenched my thirst with that good tasting ale to the point that I felt limp and sleepy. Upon arriving home, I barely had the strength to climb the several steps to the porch, where a really comfortable glider awaited me. Mom came out to greet me and remarked, "You look really tired; it must have been tough working in this heat." I responded, "You bet, Mom," as I nodded off.

I was able to buy our products at a discounted price, and I again was the favorite nephew of some of my uncles. Upon graduating from college, when teaching jobs in the area weren't readily attainable, I stayed on with that company for the next year on a full-time basis.

* * * * *

After our marriage in October 1950, I was hired by Dad to drive the town garbage collection truck. Dad had the contract to collect the town garbage. This was not one of my favorite jobs, since we collected garbage five days a week. During down times, I would clean the truck and deliver tons of coal to private residences.

CHAPTER FIFTEEN

CAREER AND FAMILY BEGINNINGS

We stayed temporarily with Ceil and Herb, and we met and were warmly greeted and welcomed to the area by their neighbors. In May, I reported to my new job at the Arsenal. In short order, we found an apartment, and Dodo found a job with a business firm in Trenton, New Jersey, a 15-minute bus commute away.

Our 3-room, unfurnished apartment was in a private, old, and charming home. It was located on Radcliffe Street, across the street from the deep-flowing Delaware River in the small town of Bristol. The town dated back to the Revolutionary days. It had its tree-lined streets; old, elegant homes along the river on Radcliffe Street; an old historic hotel, and a main street of family-owned businesses. On summer evenings, we would stroll down to the waterfront miniature park. There we would listen to musical groups, watch people fishing, or just watch heavily-gladdened ore ships being pushed upriver by tugboats to the local booming steel plant as we enjoyed the cool evening breeze coming over the water.

After four and a half years of being married, we were experiencing a serene, comfortable, yet exciting new change in our life. We were establishing new roots, and we had fun furnishing, for the first time, our own apartment. We lived about a mile or so from Ceil and Herb, and we often visited with them. We joined them and their close neighbors at their picnics and other neighborhood social activities. We also visited friends Evie and Charles, who were now residing in southwest Philadelphia about an hour away.

When I reported to the Arsenal, I was assigned to a new group that was responsible for the maintenance portion of the 2 radar systems that I had been trained on in the Army. The group was being staffed by calling people from various organizations within the Arsenal. They were mostly WWII veterans in their 30s. They had taken advantage of the GI Bill and were extremely knowledgeable and capable electronic and mechanical technicians. A few were even pursuing engineering degrees at night school.

The group had recently received their early production model of each radar system. They were developing formal maintenance and repair instructions along with technical instructions and guidance. All of this data was being disseminated to the troops, who, along with their radar systems, were going to be deployed.

Finally, we participated in developing a communications network wherein field problems could be effectively reported and responded to.

When I reported to the group, I was introduced individually to all of the members and supervisors. They all expressed a warm welcome, and some even said, "We heard you were coming on board; where have you been?" I felt a sincere feeling of acceptance. My job title was equipment specialist. I had a formal job description, but my supervisors decided to use my hands-on training and experience with radar systems to the benefit of the group. Since the group members were just beginning to be slotted for the formal 3-month training program on one or the other of the 2 systems at Aberdeen and were working from design documents, they had me conduct an informal hardware introduction program for my supervisors and colleagues. I would take 3 people at a time over to the hardware site for a few hours at a time. We would open the system's compartments, and I would point out the major components and we would discuss their contributions to the overall performance of the system. I had them sit in the operators' seats, go through the startup and operating procedures, and soon detect and track targets.

Throughout this program, I sensed that I was gaining their respect. I also conducted a compressed system operating demonstration for small groups of selected personnel and upper level managers whose organizations had different responsibilities in the systems. I was now meeting and greeting a lot of people at various levels throughout the Arsenal.

As my first year anniversary at the Arsenal approached, and the radar systems' deployment was starting to expand, I was assigned to work with a colleague and representatives of the production and quality engineering departments. As incident failure reports were starting to trickle in, we analyzed them to determine if they were random or a more serious symptom of a system wide problem that would require hardware medication. I reviewed our response to the field troops to make sure we were providing adequate details, especially in cases where we were recommending additional corrective actions.

I met and had lunch with my former Army boss, Mr. Ernie, during his periodic liaison visits to the Arsenal. During his last visit, I sincerely thanked him for his prior suggestion that I consider this perfect job opportunity and especially for his faith in me in recommending me to the people that I was now working for. He smiled and commented that in me, he felt that the troops would have a full time representative at the Arsenal who would make sure they received the adequate assistance and guidelines they might need on a timely basis. As we warmly shook hands for the last time, I assured him that I would do my best.

Meanwhile, Dodo was still working at her firm's payroll department. She was enjoying the friendly atmosphere and budding friendships with her female co-workers and had joined their local bowling team. Life was rosy; we loved our personal relationship, enjoyed our work and residential environments, and enjoyed socializing with our friends and families.

In the latter part of the summer of 1955, we were upstate attending an event at one of her relatives' houses when she began experiencing severe abdominal pains. With the help of her relatives, Dodo quickly saw a highly recommended specialist. He corrected her problem and restricted her physical and travel activity for a few days. Then, to our extreme disappointment, he told her that she would not conceive any child unless she underwent one and possibly more operations. Even then, there would only be a 50 percent chance of success. Soon after we returned home, Dodo visited our extremely knowledgeable family physician, Dr. Margoloese. He had the upstate report and conclusion. He declared her sufficiently fit to accompany me on an upcoming 8-week, work-related trip to Ohio. He gave her some pills to take, asked her to drop in after our return, and told her that with God's blessing we may have good news.

Right after our 5th anniversary, in early October, we drove to Fort Clinton. I was to assist in the system overhaul and potential upgrade program training course for selected Army Depot civilians from various locations. We found residence in town on the shore of Lake Erie, adjacent to a beautiful waterfront park. Dodo met the wife of another student who was also residing there.

During the weekdays, the girls would go shopping or explore the town while we went out to the local Army installation. On weekends, Dodo and I would tour that region of Ohio, and most often spend time at the park. There we would walk or sit around talking with locals and watching the sailboats tacking on the small river as they were leaving or returning to their sheltered mooring. Other times, we would walk over and watch the fishing boats.

We enjoyed the time we had spent in Ohio. We felt that we had experienced our second, albeit extended, honeymoon. Upon our return, Dodo visited our doctor. He checked her and happily confirmed what we had already suspected. Dodo was pregnant.

He referred us to Dr. Hyman, an obstetrician in Levittown. In those early days, as home construction rates were increasing, and more and more young, fertile couples were moving in, he would become the most popular OB in the area. He received notoriety as the baby doctor of Levittown and eventually delivered thousands of babies.

He had his own room at the hospital, where occasionally he would nap or rest between impending deliveries.

He also found the time and energy to father a bunch of his own children. A visit to his office was an experience in and of itself. Dodo would sign in at her appointed time and join an occasionally filled waiting room of women in various stages of pregnancy. The doctor was often running late because of an earlier delivery, and refreshments were available.

At one visit, after waiting there for about an hour, Dodo came out and told me that she had rescheduled her appointment because the doctor had just been called to the hospital. It was funny to see husbands outside, napping in their cars or discussing sports while waiting for their wives.

On the night of Dodo's last visit, the Doctor concluded that she was ready to go; the baby was in the proper position, and he felt that the baby only needed a nudge. He proposed that Dodo take a good dose of castor oil at midnight, but not before, and if his feelings were correct, he would see her at the hospital at a reasonable hour the next day, rather than be called in the middle of the night. At the appointed time, Dodo went into the kitchen and very soon called for me to come in and help. She was standing at the sink with a tablespoon full of oil in one hand and a huge glass of soda in the other, and she noted that we were low on juice. She asked, "Please hold my nose, because I can't stand the smell of this stuff." We stood there laughing as she made several unsuccessful attempts to raise the spoon to her lips. The doctor's feelings were correct. On July 24, 1956, Dodo gave birth at Lower Bucks Hospital to our first child, a beautiful, healthy, baby daughter we decided to name Donna.

When I brought them home, our family doctor came over, checked them both, and was pleased with their physical conditions. Since it was our first baby, he informed Dodo of what she could expect and what to watch for during our baby's growth. As he was leaving, we were all laughing as he asked us to introduce Donna and give his regards to the upstate doctor during our next visit to that area.

At Donna's baptism, we were joined by various family members. Dodo's sister Ceil and my brother Gene were the godparents.

Dodo didn't return to her former job. We shared the same deep feelings that the mother should have a full rather than a part time opportunity to nurture her unique bond with the child, especially with a daughter. I was still experiencing that feeling with my mom, while Dodo had been deprived of it at an early age with the death of her mom.

So we were now experiencing the joy and excitement of being parents. Our life was steadily progressing; we bought our first new car, and, at work, I was quickly moving up the ladder as my responsibilities expanded.

I was designated as our group representative on an Arsenal-wide team that was responsible for detecting recurring hardware problems and developing the required corrective actions. The program that we had previously developed was paying dividends and we were able to detect any recurring problems early on. As we noted any problems, the engineer determined the necessary hardware changes. The procurement and production representative negotiated contract changes with the production contractor to implement these changes into the systems and spare units coming down the production line. My group coordinated the dissemination of field change kits by select Army depots to the troops in the field. These kits included the hardware and instructions required at the troop level for implementing the changes into the fielded systems.

We all used this approach to issue changes that extended or improved the systems' capabilities and reliability. When a change was determined to be extensive, we would have the depot or the contractor implement the change at the modular level and issue these modules to the troops on a direct exchange basis.

Participation in this effort gave me an opportunity to work with members of other in- and out-of-house organizations. I learned how they effectively performed their particular areas of responsibility as they related to fielding military equipment. I would also occasionally visit production contractors and Army depot facilities to initiate or follow up on required actions that our group was generating. In fact, at one point, I took a week-long trip during which I visited Army installations at Texarkana, Huntsville, and San Francisco.

CHAPTER SIXTEEN
LEVITTOWN

As Donna's first birthday was approaching, Ceil and Herb, who had previously been transferred out of the area, decided to sell their home. We bought it, and, in July of 1957, moved into our own home at 11 Copper Beech Lane in Levittown, Pennsylvania.

Our one-story, 3-bedroom, 1-bath home was located in the Crabtree section, one of the earliest-built sections, wherein all of the street names began with the letter "C." All of the homes in our immediate vicinity were identical inside, with only slight variations on the outside.

We had met and socialized with our neighbors during our prior short stay and the frequent follow up visits with Ceil and Herb. We were quickly adopted as friends.

Most of our neighbors were in their 30's, and many of the men were World War II veterans. They came from various areas, including New York, New Jersey, Philadelphia, and upstate Pennsylvania. They moved into their new homes in a new community where job opportunities were plentiful and the environment was great for raising a family. They freely helped one another on projects and especially in emergencies and enjoyed social and sports activities. Visiting with one another was a frequent and natural event.

The men loved sports. We would discuss them over a can of beer, or we would play horseshoes in the backyard. We would occasionally go to the high school football game, and we enjoyed jointly watching pro football games on TV, especially our favorite team, the Eagles.

The women enjoyed their coffee breaks and would discuss the latest fashions, food recipes, and rearing children.

The highlight of our social activities was our picnics and parties. They were hosted by our next door neighbors, Lydia and Jack, who were centrally located and had a large side patio with a large fireplace. Along with hot dogs and hamburgers, the women would prepare their special dishes and desserts, and the men would prepare the drinks, including whiskey sours and pina coladas. Jack would proudly serve his favorite, delicious, homemade baked beans, which he had spent the previous day preparing.

* * * * *

This was a neighborhood of friends, and our closest friendship developed with Lydia and Jack. We were the youngest couple in the group; Jack was a couple years older than the other three of us, was a WWII Army veteran, and had participated in the D-Day invasion of Europe and the Battle of the Bulge at the age of 21.

The four of us had more in common than just our ages; we were all born and grew up in small upstate towns; we shared a compatible sense of values, humor, customs, and entertainment, and we had all been married in 1950.

We were all upstate college graduates. Jack and Lydia had met and begun dating while attending Mansfield College in Lydia's hometown, where Jack had been matriculating under the GI Bill. Three of us had teaching certificates, but only Jack was actively pursuing that profession. He quickly became a principal at one of our local elementary schools.

We loved sports, and both Jack and I had participated in them at both the high school and college levels. Jack was a big man and was an outstanding football lineman at the tackle position.

We enjoyed going out to dinner on special occasions, and we really enjoyed our Friday night pinochle games. It was the men versus the women, and we would talk, drink, and eat desserts as we played and relaxed for several hours.

* * * * *

The most rewarding event in the neighborhood, though, was the family enlargement. There were quite a few youngsters of various ages, and it seemed that every year, someone was expecting a new baby.

We participated in that event when, in 1959, Dodo became pregnant for the second time, this time without the help of the pill. Her visits with Dr. Hayman, whose office was now only two blocks from our home, were a repeat of her prior visits, but were more unpredictable, because his practice was expanding.

On November 29, 1959, without the aid of castor oil, Dodo gave birth at Lower Bucks Hospital to our second child, another healthy, beautiful daughter. We decided to name her Diane.

Mom and Dad and various family members and friends joined us at her baptism, where Dodo's sister Belle and my brother Ron were the godparents. We had experienced the unknown of nurturing a baby with the birth of our first child, so now we were more experienced and relaxed as we enjoyed our new baby.

Then, on December 8, 1963, Dodo gave birth to our third child, another healthy, beautiful daughter. We decided to name her Janet. During her delivery, Dr. Hayman was simultaneously assisting an adjoining woman as she was also delivering. I brought Dodo and Janet home in a couple of days; my parents returned to their upstate home, and we resumed our preparations for Christmas.

Two weeks after giving birth, Dodo began experiencing abdominal pains which rapidly became severe. Lydia ran over to take care of our children as I rushed Dodo to the hospital, where Dr. Hayman was waiting to meet us. After examining her, he told me that she was in very serious condition and suffering from an extreme post natal infection. He was cautiously optimistic that she would recover, but she would be hospitalized for a week or so to ensure her complete recovery.

On that late night drive home, I was praying and asking God to help her recover and keep her from meeting the same fate that her mother had under similar circumstances. I was also crying, for her and for our daughters, as I realized that they weren't going to share her birthday celebration and the joy and excitement of opening presents on Christmas morning.

My parents came right back down to tend to the kids. I spent the next day, Christmas Eve, her birthday, visiting with her at the now quiet and relatively evacuated hospital. Her condition was stabilizing, and she was showing slight signs of improvement. She teared up when the kids called excitedly wishing her a happy birthday, and I noted her determination to overcome her problem.

We were making up a list of the kids' gifts that were wrapped and hidden in the attic when we heard a choral group out in the hall, stopping at the few occupied rooms, to sing Christmas carols. They were a well-intentioned group, but their action served to drive home the sadness of our situation. I stepped out and asked that they not stop at our room, and they understood.

That night, after Mom and I finally put the two older excited kids to bed, Dad went outside for a walk in the few inches of freshly fallen snow, and I sat on the floor sorting and placing the gifts under the tree.

Diane, 4 years old at the time, came running out of their bedroom, crying, laughing, and excitedly telling me that Santa was just outside her window. He said he was checking on the children and would be back with their gifts after they fell asleep. It took me a while to calm her down, dissuade her insistence, and get her back to bed. Dad came in and told me that he had only been trying to get her to go to sleep as he passed her window.

The girls were excited opening their gifts the next morning. As soon as Diane opened her last gift, she insisted on going outside to look at the snow. She came right back in; took my hand, and said, "Come on, Dad; I want to show you something that you have to see." She led me out, pointed to the ground, and jubilantly said, "That's Santa's footprints; I told you the truth last night. He was outside my window." I said, "Yes, honey, I guess he was."

Dodo recovered quickly, and in a few days, I brought her back home. My parents and other family members and friends joined us at Janet's baptism, where my sister Andrea and Dodo's brother Vince were the godparents. We were enjoying our new baby as spring was approaching, and life settled back to normal.

* * * * *

As our children grew, we enjoyed watching them play and invent their own games with their friends. Occasionally, we would join in and introduce them to games that we had played and invented in our youth.

During the hula hoop fad, Jack and I were totally unsuccessful in getting the knack of swiveling the hoop around our hips, but our wives were much better at it. When we men tried it, the kids would laugh and give us thumbs down. I recalled how we, as kids, had played with different types of barrel rings that we would salvage. I straightened out and shaped a metal clothes hanger and used its hook to propel and maneuver the hula hoop. Jack and the kids were applauding and giving me thumbs up as I demonstrated my prowess by bouncing the hoop up and down the curb and doing figure 8's in the street.

Our neighbor stopped in the midst of cutting his lawn, and joined us to demonstrate his hula hoop skills. As he was doing so, his short, boisterous, visiting New York mother-in-law, got up off her knees and told him that she would not tolerate her 40-year-old son-in-law playing with a hula hoop while she was weeding the flower beds. He departed, murmuring that he couldn't wait for her to leave as we expressed our sympathy.

Dodo and I tried to introduce our daughters to our way life through a blend of appropriate seriousness and light hearted fun. They would help Dodo with household chores and after-dinner clean up. They would help me to plant and then harvest vegetables and flowers, and they learned the difference between weeds and productive plants. We, as did our neighbors, had a peach tree that produced the juiciest, sweetest, and largest fruits imaginable, and we would enjoy gorging ourselves during the short harvest season.

We took our daughters to our local pool, where they would splash and began learning how to swim, and they would help in decorating our home for the various holidays. They helped me raise and fly our country flag on appropriate occasions, and we all enjoyed watching our local holiday parades, especially after Donna began marching and twirling a baton, in the front row of the youngest section of the Belles and Beaus baton twirling group. On the Fourth of July, we would sit on a house roof to view the fireworks display emanating from our local church carnival.

When Donna was 4 years old, I held her up on my shoulders, amidst a huge crowd at our local shopping center, to see JFK as he campaigned for the presidency.

Several years later, we watched his funeral on TV, and, a few years after that, we all stood at our local train station, holding hands, to pay our respects to Robert Kennedy's funeral train as it slowly passed on its way to our nation's capital.

* * * * *

While residing in Levittown, my progression at work was better and more rapid than we could have hoped for. In early 1959, not quite five years after starting at the Arsenal at the lowest grade, in my unit, I was promoted to a first line supervisory position. I was now technically supervising seven equipment specialists in providing logistical and technical support to Army units that were using and maintaining a family of anti-aircraft fire control systems. Even though subordinates had all preceded me into our unit and were older, each one of them extended their heartfelt congratulations and full support.

Two years later, in 1961, I spent ten months as our division member on an arsenal study group. I worked with R&D engineers in developing a concept for an electronic, multi-purpose automatic inspection and diagnostic system (MAIDS), wherein we could test the operational status of various families of Army operational equipment. I concentrated on developing the concept to test the family of Army anti-aircraft missile systems, while my colleagues concentrated on tank and automotive engines. I had taken a guided missile management course at Redstone Arsenal in Huntsville, Alabama, (responsible agency). During our study, I had visited them a couple of times to confirm that my findings and conclusions that this type of testing of guided missile systems was technically possible.

We widely disseminated our study group report and findings, received funding, and assembled and installed a pilot test system in a depot in Pennsylvania to test tank engines returned there for repair. The system basically consisted of a dynamometer, transducers, control panel, a computer, and a printer that detailed the test results, engine performance, and, if necessary, the location of repair instructions. The system exceeded our expectations, received notoriety by reducing labor and costs, and was demonstrated to numerous visiting dignitaries.

The computer that was used in the test system was the "Field Artillery Digital Automatic Computer," commonly referred to as FADAC. The FADAC was in the final development phase by the Arsenal. The FADAC was scheduled to be deployed to field artillery units wherein, after inputting variable data, it would determine the correct gun firing position. Analog computers were large and hard wired, and their major components were the multitude heat generating, relatively short-lived vacuum tubes. FADAC, on the other hand, was a compact unit (as high as a bread box and roughly three times the size) and portable. It contained approximately one hundred roughly 4 x 6 inch printed circuit cards that contained the more reliable and longer lived diodes and transistors, and it had an 8,000-word rotating disc memory with read and write heads. Digital computers were still in the embryonic stage, their potential yet to be explored, and here again the Army gave me the opportunity to get in on the ground floor of this new technology.

The next year, 1962, I was designated the division project leader for FADAC and planned and coordinated the schedule for logistic support plans, new equipment training, and technical manuals in preparation for its upcoming deployment. Two years later, in May 1964, my ten-year anniversary at the Arsenal, as the Vietnam War was expanding, I was promoted to senior engineering technician in a system engineering position in the Commodity Management Office of the Arsenal commanding officer's staff. There were 10 of us in that office, 8 of whom had engineering degrees. Two of us had equivalent grade and stature, and each of us had management and oversight responsibilities at the command level for several critical fire control systems. This designation was applied to systems urgently needed by the Army; that were high profile, or that were experiencing technical, scheduled, cost, or operational problems in the field.

We exercised our management responsibility by conducting frequent system team meetings with involved Arsenal organization team representatives. In these meetings, we would identify the problem areas and recommend and, at times, direct appropriate corrective action to be taken by involved organizational elements (i.e. development and production engineering, quality assurance, procurement, production, and logistical support) to ensure satisfaction of commitments to customers, (i.e., various branches of the Army). Finally, we would provide written weekly reports and periodic briefings to the commander and other, higher commanders denoting our progress and the problem areas with the associated corrective actions that were being taken.

One of the items assigned to me was FADAC, the computer that was by then in the initial production and deployment phase. We started receiving failure reports to the degree that they degraded the system reliability factor to borderline acceptable. Our team quality engineer analyzed the reports, found the failures to be random in nature, but also noted that over ninety percent of them occurred during the first 40 hours of the computer's operation. We immediately negotiated a change order with our production contractor requiring a 40-hour run-in on every computer before shipment, and the reliability factor shot way up.

While managing the FADAC program, I participated with our contract officer in formulating the procurement philosophy and the evaluation factors that our survey team would use to determine if a prospective production contractor could produce the items in accordance with the contract requirements. These factors included determining if the contractor had adequate production and test facilities, and associated trained and experienced personnel, quality assurance program, engineering staff, and management, and support organizations.

I also chaired our survey team of representatives from the various organizational elements and visited the prospective contractors' facilities to evaluate all of the factors, following which we would give our recommendation to our contract officer to award or not to award the contract.

There was an amusing incident that happened when I led the survey team to a prospective contractor's facility in a town in northeast Pennsylvania, in close, proximity to my hometown. After the initial briefing by management and lead staff, we took an oversight tour of the facility. As we were touring the departments, I kept hearing an endearing greeting of "Hi, Breezy" and even heard one shout of, "Hey, Breezy, what the hell you doin' here?" As I acknowledged the greetings, I noticed a smile on the faces of management and my team members, one of whom said,

"What's with this Breezy shit?" I explained that was my nickname, that everyone in the area called me that, and that these were greetings from relatives friends, and former classmates. I recused myself from the team discussions of evaluating factors. The team recommended the award; the contractor met all contract requirements, delivered quality products on time, and was the successful low bidder on subsequent contracts.

There were various social events held at the Arsenal, and Dodo and I attended some of them, including family picnics, Christmas parties, and occasional command level functions. I bowled in a league at the Arsenal alleys where I maintained a 180 average. In one game, I started with 7 strikes and rolled 267 for one of the highest scores rolled at the Arsenal alleys.

CHAPTER SEVENTEEN

FAMILY VISITS AND VACTIONS

While living in Levittown, we began a tradition of visiting and socializing with our families during the various seasons of the year. We visited with my parents on Thanksgiving, during Christmas week, and at Easter. We were joined occasionally by my siblings who would also return to the area for a visit. We would exchange gifts, share a blessed wafer, and spend a day family skiing at Christmas. At the Easter, visit we would dye eggs, have the food basket blessed that we shared at Easter breakfast, and engage in the traditional cracking of eggs.

Mom loved canaries and always had one in her home. One spring, she decided to mate them. When Dodo and I and the girls arrived for our visit, she proudly pointed to the mating cage, its two inhabitants, and the nest they had built, and she expressed her disappointment that nothing had happened yet, though she still held out hope.

That night, after everyone had gone to bed, I was at the table having a late snack. I was pondering if there was anything I could do to stimulate those birds to take action.

There on the table sat an Easter basket filled with jelly beans. My conscience said, "Don't you even think about it." The devil in me said "Hey yes, do it." The devil won. I had no idea what the color of canary eggs was, but I sifted through the jelly beans and picked out two white, dull beans, placed them in the nest, and went up to bed.

The next morning, I came down, and there was Mom, Dodo, and the girls, all with smiles on their faces. Mom said, "They were busy last night." I looked over and there was that stupid canary, sitting on and trying to hatch those jelly beans. I smiled and said, "Looks that way Mom."

Shortly, the canary vacated the nest. Mom scurried to the cage for a close-up look and said, "She was really busy last night; there's two eggs." The girls were cheering, and I was having trouble controlling my facial expressions. Mom quickly got a quizzical look on her face and began looking back and forth between me and the cage. She removed one of the beans from the nest, and then asked me, "Would you know anything about this?" I responded, "Mom, why would you ask that?" She responded, "I gave you life; you're my son, and I know you." As we were all laughing, she asked, "What gave you that idea?" I replied, "I'm your son, Mom, and you also gave me your sense of humor."

After we returned home, Mom called and said the jelly bean idea worked, because the mating effort was successful. Soon thereafter, Mom gave us our first young canary, and Dodo and the girls decided that he should be called Sonny Boy.

* * * * *

In the early afternoon on Christmas Day, we would depart on a 3-hour drive to Belle and Johnny's in Connecticut for Dodo's family Christmas gathering. We would be joined by other family members who lived in the same general area.

Johnny was an energetic, hardworking young man who owned and operated a highly successful grocery store. It was located in the wealthiest county in Connecticut, and he featured top grade meat cuts and other top level products. In time, he acquired an adjoining liquor store.

Belle and Johnny would host the gathering at their spacious home that was situated on a seven acre property with a beautiful pond in the rolling hills of Connecticut. They would prepare and serve a luscious, mouthwatering, family-style dinner, frequently prime rib accompanied by her exotic Lebanese salad, called tubule, that was one of my favorites. There would be a constant flow of top shelf wines and various mixed adult drinks.

Our contributions to the gathering were boxes of delicious homemade Christmas cookies that Dodo had spent the previous several weeks preparing, baking, and hiding from me and the girls, along with Dodo's deliciously famous homemade poppy seed and walnut sweet bread loafs. We were well into our trip one year when Dodo said, "Oh-oh, we have to go back home." When I asked her what we had left on, she replied, "It's worse than that; we forgot the cookies and bread." We quickly concluded that time wouldn't permit us to go back. Dodo was upset and really disappointed that her family wouldn't be able to share her cookies that they expected and really enjoyed. The girls and I also expressed our disappointment but also reveled, as we anticipated gorging on those cookies and bread upon our return home.

Christmas in the Connecticut countryside was always a warm, picturesque scene. The homes were widely spaced across the terrain, and, along with the properties, were elegantly decorated. Some years, the ponds and lakes were frozen, and the ground was covered with freshly fallen snow that added a clean beauty and quiet serenity.

The years we experienced the latter conditions, the girls took along their ice skates. On Christmas night, they joined with their cousins and, led by Dennis, built a bonfire at the pond. They took to the ice, skating, playing games, and having fun, as they strengthened their friendships and family relationships.

Some of us adults joined them around the fire, sipping our hot drinks and happily watching the bonding of our next generation. Occasionally, we would encounter light snow falling that enhanced the beauty and reverence of the scene. Seemingly, all too soon, Christmas Day would be over. On the return trip home the next day, we would rehash the joy and excitement of another family gathering.

Occasionally, we couldn't attend one of these gatherings. One year, the northeast was hit with a surprise heavy snowfall on Christmas Eve, and overnight into Christmas Day. A trip to Connecticut was out of the question. Dodo and I were talking, and she was pondering as to what she could prepare for our Christmas dinner, since we hadn't anticipated being home. I suggested a dinner of cookies. She laughed and frowned as she said, "That figures." There was a knock at the door, and there stood our snow-laden neighbor's daughter. She held a bowl of baked beans in one hand, and in the other she held a turkey neck, wrapped in a red ribbon and bow, with a note attached. It said, "Merry Christmas; please join use for dinner, Lydia & Jack." They shared their dinner with us, and we shared our cookies and bread with them.

* * * * *

In 1957, we and Dodo's youngest sister, Evie, and her husband, Steve, decided that we and our infant children would spend our 2 week summer vacation together. The four of us were within 3 years of age with compatible personalities. Steve and I were well on our way to developing a close, respectful, brotherly relationship.

Steve was born and raised in New York City. He earned an appointment to, and graduated from, the U.S. Coast Guard Academy, where he received a mechanical engineering degree and a naval officer commission.

While serving his subsequent three-year tour of duty, he met Evie at the public health service hospital on Staten Island. Also a commissioned naval officer, she had been stationed there as a dietitian following her graduation from Penn State. Following their marriage and subsequent discharge from the service, they relocated to Connecticut. Steve was employed at United Aircraft Corp. working on aircraft engine design.

That year we, along with their 1 ½-year-old son, Steven, and our 1-year-old daughter, Donna, rented a two-story lake front cottage on Lake Sheridan in northeast Pennsylvania. It was about a 30-minute drive from our hometown, and we had spent some time there in our youth. It was one of several lakes that were in close proximity to the small rural town of Fleetville.

The town had one intersection with a blinking traffic light and an old general store; a tavern, a combination gas station; post office, a grange hall, and a volunteer fire company. The town also had a municipal airport, which was nothing more than a wind sock on a pole, at one end of an unused cow pasture. Lastly, it had the Lakeland Golf Course. The golf course had a nine hole, executive length, par 3 layout that sat on what used to be a cow pasture.

After we unpacked our cars that first year, Steve and I toured the home. During the tour, he noticed that the kitchen sink, instead of having faucets, had a manually operated long handled pump that brought up underground water. He was opening and closing the doors to the various rooms and turned to me with a stunned look on his face and said, "We don't have a bathroom."

I said, "Yes, we do; it's that shed next to the gate with a half-moon cutout in the door. It's called an outhouse."

"You've got to be kidding," he said. "I've never seen one, never mind used one." He roared as I said, "It's easy; you'll get used to it. Just use the correct-sized hole."

The next morning, as I was walking out with a correspondence course document in my hand, Steve was astonished as he asked, "Are you going to read in there?"

I replied, "Sure, it's quiet and peaceful and a great place to study."

Later that day, as Steve was going out with his arm tight to his side, he said, "I'm going to give it a try." I asked him what he had under his arm, and we both laughed as he exposed the spray can containing lilac scented air freshener.

We had fun on that vacation, using the outhouse, bathing in the lake, visiting my parents, where we could take a hot shower, and manually pumping our water.

The next year, we returned and were joined by David, their nine-month-old son. He gave us a scare late one night when he developed a severe case of croup. We fired up the stove and filled all the pots that we could find. As the steam built up, we used blankets in a makeshift tent to confine the steam, and we were able to relieve his condition.

After a couple of years of this routine, we began a long period of renting a cottage from friends of Evie. It was located at Hansom Lake on the opposite side of town. We were joined by our new daughters, their Pam and our Diane. Some four years later, we were again joined by new daughters, their Cindy and our Janet.

To get to the cottage, we would turn off a dirt road and onto a lane that adjoined a farm house. We would proceed through a pasture, where we would open and close a big gate. After avoiding ruts and large, embedded rocks, we would arrive at the cottage, where we would make several trips down a steep and awkward set of railroad tie steps, carrying our luggage to the lower-level lakefront cottage. It was a single-story, four-bedroom cottage. It had a fireplace in the living room, and in the kitchen area it had a gas/coal stove and a sink with hot and cold faucets.

At the waterfront, there was a patio and fireplace, a dock, an offshore anchored float, a boat, and a canoe. Best of all, close to the house, there was a shed that contained the bathroom, a shower stall, and an outdoor refrigerator where we would store our beer, soda, and gallons of drinking water that we filled from a local, constantly-flowing spring pipe.

Steve was a strong, excellent swimmer, and the kids observed his proper techniques as they developed their own skills. Janet became a strong swimmer, and about the age of 9 or 10 she entered a swimming contest that was sponsored by the homeowner association. She blew away the competitors in her age group as we all cheered. She had a smile of accomplishment on her face as she awaited her trophy. Her expression quickly turned to shock, and she had difficulty controlling her emotions as the judges disqualified and denied her the trophy in response to the runner-up's parents' complaint that "She was only a renter." We held our own award ceremony later that day and presented her with a bigger and nicer trophy. That brought back her smile.

We showed the kids how to propel and control the boat and canoe. Soon, two of them would be sitting alongside one another, laughing as they rowed around the lake in an unsynchronized zigzag pattern, while towing one of the others atop an inflated tire tube tethered to the boat.

They learned how to bait the hook and catch and release the numerous pan fish. Early on, we had difficulty keeping them supplied with enough night crawlers, so we improvised and bought blocks of American cheese that we diced into small cubes for easy storage. It was fun watching them walk down to the dock, carrying their paper plates laden with cheese. At the sound of their footsteps on the dock, the fish would dart in from all directions and float with their tails fanning out. The fish loved the cheese, and, for that matter, so did the kids. Soon it was one for the fish and two or more for them.

When they tired of unhooking fish, they would sprawl out on the dock and hang over the side of the dock or float in the water. They developed a fairly successful technique, wherein they would take turns dropping the cheese into the water and then net the fish as it fed. They became very selective as they competed to net the largest fish, and our dock rapidly became the lake's fish feeding station.

They enjoyed playing games, especially the ones they made up. David loved playing cowboys, and would lead them galloping up and down the hills of our usually unoccupied corner of the lake. He had them slapping their hips as they rode their make believe horses made of mops, brooms, and fallen tree limbs. When they came to the road, they would occasionally rest the horses while they picked ripe blackberries. Sometimes they would even bring us some.

A short distance from our cottage, a strip of farm land extended to the lakeshore. The kids would call out to us, "Here come the cows!" as twenty or so dairy cows would come down to the lake to refresh and relieve themselves.

The kids had three things in common: Energy, imagination, and hunger. They would usually prepare their own breakfast from the variety of cereal boxes on the counter and line up to assemble their favorite bologna and cheese sandwiches for lunch. Mid-afternoon, they would enjoy snacks on the float while taking a break from their activities. By dinnertime, they would be starving.

We adults would often join them for their waterfront activities. We would drift atop inflated floats, prior to our late afternoon cocktail hour.

We would prepare many of our meals on the outdoor grill, serve them on paper plates, and eat at the sheltered picnic tables that overlooked the lake. We had what the kids called special nights, where we would serve pizza or clams (that we steamed by the hundreds, and never seemed to have enough of), and spaghetti, which we would eat before most of the sauce soaked into the paper plates. As our staple vegetable, we would eat the locally grown sweet corn, which we would select from a stack in the general store or from a local farmhouse porch, and pay for by depositing 50 cents per dozen in the nearby copper can.

At night, when the kids were relaxing prior to going to bed, we adults would frequently play board games, particularly Clue. The kids would giggle and mimic us as they called out, "It was Col. Mustard with a wrench in the study; no, it was Mrs. Peacock with a knife in the bedroom."

After the kids were in bed, I would occasionally go out in the boat, drifting along the shoreline, surface fishing for bass that were coming in to feed. Some nights, Dodo would join me on the porch that overlooked the lake, and we would gaze at the myriad of stars in the dark sky, listen to the frogs croaking, and listen to the telltale splash of a larger fish trying to feed on the frogs and pan fish.

It was enjoyable watching the young ones having fun, growing up, and bonding, and these times provided us with some really good, teary-eyed laughs.

* * * * *

One night, the three oldest, who were all around the age of 12, decided that Donna would conduct a séance. As they were secluding themselves in the narrow, smallest bedroom, they concluded that the four younger girls shouldn't participate, because they were too young to understand or might get scared.

As I was coming back from the detached bathroom, I heard Donna's soft voice emanating through the open window. She was asking repeatedly, "Do you hear me?" I went over and placed my face in the window while simultaneously switching the spotlight on under my chin. In a low voice, I responded repeatedly, "I hear you." Their screams were instantaneous and continuous as they escaped from the room, leaving the door hanging on its hinges.

As I came into the cottage, the four younger girls came out of their bedroom to see what the excitement was all about. Dodo was looking quizzically at me. Steve was trying to calm the boys as they were breathlessly, excitedly, and repeatedly proclaiming, "She did it; she contacted Martin Luther King, Jr." As they were describing how she did it, I finally asked them, "Did he sound like this?" as I repeated my outdoor response. They froze in shock as we all enjoyed a good laugh.

* * * * *

When Diane and Pam, the middle age pairing, were about 11 years old, they decided to camp out one night. They wanted to do it all on their own, including erecting the pup tent and preparing their own breakfast. The next morning, they told us that they had had a lot of fun, but that there had been a horrible smell whose source they couldn't find. We told them it was understandable, since they had erected the tent right on top of the septic tank. In their defense, they explained that that was the only place that the ground was soft and the grass was lush.

* * * * *

Our vacation occasionally coincided with the Fleetville Fire Company annual carnival. We would attend and enjoy the local food, and the kids would ride the amusement rides and sit on the fire truck.

One year, there was a gala celebration that featured a parade of fire trucks from the surrounding area. The three oldest kids were spending the summer in Georgia, working for their Aunt Toni, so we adults and our four younger girls went into town to view the parade. As we were all sitting on the step of the general store, awaiting the parade, the local fire truck stopped at the intersection. The girls were cheering and waving to the fire personnel. Another in turn responded by inviting the girls to ride in the parade, atop the truck. They scrambled aboard, all excited, as the truck departed to the start line. Shortly, the parade arrived, and there were our big city girls riding atop the lead truck, waving to the cheering viewers, including us, and having an exciting time in this small rural community.

* * * * *

Occasionally, I would take the kids on a tour of the surrounding area. We would go to see their deceased, great-grandmother's farm, an area I had frequented in my youth. We would often stop at the Montdale Dairy, where the kids would take what seemed like forever to decide which of the 15 or so posted flavors they wanted to try.

One year, I offered to take the kids to Watkins Glen in nearby New York, but they graciously declined my offer. A couple of days later, the three eldest, who were in their teens, learned that there was a rock concert called Woodstock underway at a farm in upstate New York, and they pleaded with me to take them there. Being unfamiliar with the goings on at these concerts, I briefly contemplated their request before deciding not to go, to their disappointment.

The following Sunday, we were having a late breakfast at a country restaurant, in a rural community, at an exit off I-81, when a psychedelic painted VW minibus, with side window curtains, pulled into the parking area. In a few moments, a few matted hair, dope smoking types entered the restaurant. They were wearing bandanas, torn and soiled jeans, beads, and sandals, and they looked like they hadn't bathed in a week. We and the locals were shocked by this sight, and I was elated that I had refused the kids' request.

* * * * *

Our most enjoyable activity away from the lake was playing golf at the Lakeland Golf Course. The course was built on and incorporated the sloping contours of what used to be a cow pasture, and the hole lengths varied from one to two hundred yards. There was not a level fairway, or green, and a few of the latter had depressions running through them. We had fun playing our shots and putts off the sides of the sloping hills. The cost to play a round was 50 cents, and, if needed, an iron, putter, and ball would be provided.

When the kids were really young, they would walk along with us, carrying a club or two, swing at fallen apples, and anticipate their treat at the clubhouse. When they became big enough to swing the clubs adequately, they joined in the play.

In time, we had three groups going off the tees, with us adults going last so we could oversee and, if necessary, speed up the group ahead of us. When they reached the 9th fairway, there was no need to urge them on, for the clubhouse was in sight and they were anticipating their cold sodas.

When we adults would arrive at the clubhouse, the kids would be tallying and comparing their score cards. Some would be sipping their sodas, while others would still be at the soda machine trying to decide on what flavor they desired.

On the way back to the cottage, we would occasionally stop to refill our jugs with cold spring water, but we always stopped at the general store to pick up our staples of bread, bologna, cheese, and corn. The kids would dash into the store, head to the comic book stand, and stand there for what seemed like forever, trying to decide what books they wanted to buy, read, and share.

* * * * *

During our summer vacations, we were occasionally visited by our siblings, former hometown friends, and current neighborhood friends. But every year, Mom and Dad would spend a day with us, during which time we would have a cake and candles and would celebrate Mom's birthday. She would pretend to be surprised.

Seemingly all too soon, our summer vacation would be over. After packing our cars and saying our goodbye, we would drive out through the gated pasture. The girls would be waving goodbye, mooing to the cows, and discussing what they were going to do at the lake the next summer.

CHAPTER EIGHTEEN
OUR NEW HOME

(Section A)

As 1968 was being rung in, our daughters were growing up. Donna was nearing her teen years; the girls were sharing two bedrooms with limited closet space, and the five of us were sharing one bathroom. Dodo and I recognized and were discussing the need to either expand our home or shop for a larger one.

While on a family scouting ride one Sunday, we came across model homes that were part of a newly planned development only minutes from our residence. We toured them and found one very appealing. It was a 2-story colonial style with 4 bedrooms, 2 ½ bathrooms and central air conditioning. On the first floor it had a kitchen, dining room, living room, and den. We learned that only 30 of the roughly 300 lots to be developed were in the adjacent township, Falls, where there was a much lower tax rate and an excellent school system.

On Valentine's Day, twenty-one years to the day that Dodo and I had agreed to go steady, we wished each other happy Valentine's Day as we signed the sale agreement to buy our first new home. We chose a lot in Falls Township, a half block from the Pennsbury school district complex that contained the elementary, middle, and high schools. We subsequently sold our old home and agreed on a date in mid-August to complete the transactions on both homes, so that our kids could start the school year attending their new schools.

During the spring and early summer, we frequently visited our lot to see and check the construction progress on our new home. By mid-August, our house was essentially completed; however, the installation of the underground utilities was behind schedule and would take at least another month to complete. The buyer of our old home agreed to delay the settlement to the end of August. Our home builder proposed that we move in at that time, rent free, and gave us a key to use the model home, in the evenings, to take our showers and obtain water for the next day. Being adventurous and not seeing any better options, we, with our lawyer's approval, agreed to the builder's offer.

On moving day, the van backed in from Hood Boulevard, through two adjacent undeveloped lots. The boulevard was the outer perimeter of our section of the development, which, on the opposite side of the street, had the school complex. On our side, there were a couple of homes completed and occupied. We were the first to move in on our street which, at this point, was just dirt, as was our driveway. As we were unloading the van and placing the furniture, the girls were unpacking boxes, handling clothes, and marveling as they each moved in to their own bedroom.

The last items removed from the van were our queen-sized bedding. Lo and behold, our rigid box spring was an inch or two too wide to clear one of the points on the stairway. The builder corrected the problem the next day, but on that first night, Dodo and I were arranging our bedding on the living room floor when she laughed and said, "This is ironic; our kids are sleeping in their own beds and here we are preparing to spend our first night in our new, beautiful home sleeping on the floor."

For the next several weeks, we established a reasonable routine. I went to work, the kids reported to school on the first day, including Janet, who actually was a day too early for kindergarten and who spent the day helping the teacher prepare the classroom for the next day's start. Dodo unpacked our belongings, did the necessary daily food shopping and washed our laundry at the local laundromat. The kids did their homework as they came in from school and then went out to play with their new friends in our sparsely occupied area. Dodo prepared our meals on a camper stove and, late in the evening, we took our showers in the model home. The kids never complained; they were having fun treating our situation as an adventure.

During the first half of September, the crews made an all-out effort and completed installing and connecting us to the various utilities. By the first week in October, the construction crews had completed the installation of our driveway, the sidewalks, and the curbs, and had applied the base coat to the street.

On October 10, 1968, three days after our 18th wedding anniversary, Dodo and I went to settlement, and officially became the owners of our new home at 705 Warwick Road, in Fairless Hills. House construction in the rest of the development was accelerating, and soon some houses were being completed and occupied, while others were being started. Within 18 months or so, all of the homes were completed and occupied by new neighbors.

* * * * *

It was during this period that we experienced a stunning, unexpected family loss. Dodo's sister Ceil died from a brain aneurysm. Following their mom's death, it was Ceil who played a major role in raising Dodo and giving her moral support and guidance, up to and well through her formative teenage years. Dodo was devastated, and, one night, as she let her emotions flow, she noted that this was the fourth of her immediate family to die. Previously, Mom, Dad, and brother Ted had died. Three of the four of them had died before the age of 50. For the first and only time, Dodo told me that "Life isn't fair," but her deep faith gradually helped her overcome this emotional setback.

Our emotions also swung to the positive end of the scale, when, in July 1969, we, along with the rest of the country, watched on TV with joy and pride as the first human, American astronaut Neil Armstrong, stepped onto and walked on the surface of the moon and returned safely. Mom and Dad were amazed, recounting their youth in the horse and buggy days, as they watched a human walk on the moon. A few years later, we watched President Nixon resign from office in disgrace over his role in a cover-up of a minor crime.

* * * * *

As the pioneers on our street, Dodo and I introduced ourselves as Dodo and Breezy and greeted and welcomed our new neighbors. We found an interesting age mix among them. There was the over-45 group, mostly WWII vets, who, like us, were moving from Levittown into larger homes to accommodate growing families and into a more efficiently run township, with its low tax rate and close proximity to the excellent school system where they could enroll their children.

The other group consisted of those who were 35 and younger. They were in the beginning stages of expanding and raising families and were buying their first new homes.

The two age groups were united in their desire to create a warm, cooperative, and secure neighborhood wherein they could raise their families.

Many of the women were stay-at-home moms, and the men worked in their various professions. We had a minister, a local newspaper editor, a couple of doctors and engineers, a restaurant manager, an industrial construction company co-owner, a plumber, a steel mill foreman, an over the road trucker, and a garment manufacturer. They willingly and routinely shared their knowledge and offered their help in their areas of expertise.

Dodo and I, now entering our 40s, found ourselves as the youngest of the older group and the oldest of the younger group. Some of the younger women, new to the area, would drop in during the day and ask Dodo about the location and reputation of facilities that they were considering patronizing. Some would drop in for a cup of coffee, a chat, or to discuss a problem they were experiencing. They would confide in her because they sensed her trustworthiness. She, in essence, became their older sister, and their young children respectfully called us as Aunt Dodo and Uncle Breezy.

Dodo and several of the women joined a bowling league, and we husbands enjoyed accompanying them to their Christmas and end of the year awards banquets. We would lead the cheering and clapping when they won awards. She started a very active quilting club that met at least once a week, and she and the other experienced women introduced the novices to the art of quilting.

The first quilt that they made was in our living room. The women would gather, and they would quilt and talk, snack and talk, and drink and talk even more. We got our second canary, as a gift from Mom, and we named him Stash. He had a powerful voice and an extensive range, and loved to sing when people talked. As the women talked, he would begin singing. As they raised their voices, so did he. Finally, they would move him out of the hall and place the night cover on his cage, where you could still hear his muffled singing, but at a tolerable level.

Our French poodle, Beauregard Brummell, whom we called Beau, enjoyed relaxing on the landing midway up our stairway. He would seemingly tire of the high noise level and would join me in the den or head for his bed in the garage. The women would end the night enjoying a delicious, homemade dessert, which I was also looked forward to and which they would let me share. They would still be talking as they left.

* * * * *

Beau was a one-year-old, medium-sized French poodle when my brother Ron gave him to us as a gift. Ron had owned him for a year and taught him many tricks, some of which I had to break him of. Among other traits, Beau fashioned himself as a protector and a sentry. His ears and head would pop up, and he would give out a couple of barks whenever he heard footsteps or unfamiliar voices outside our home.

One night, Beau gave out a couple of barks that awoke us. I went to the window, where I saw and heard a couple of young people in the street heading toward our driveway and saying, "Let's try this one; it looks like no one's home." Beau really started barking then, and they quickly back tracked and headed up the street while Dodo was on the phone relaying the events to the police. Soon the police came up the street with their lights and sirens turned off, followed the footprints in the snow, and arrested the culprits as they were carrying a TV out from a neighbor's home. Beau became a neighborhood hero.

One of the neighborhood couples, Arlene and Toni, had an older female French poodle named Babette that they wanted to have mated before she grew too old. Beau, with his pedigree papers, was selected for the honor. All of the women felt that it would be crude for the dogs to just meet and mate, and concluded that it would be more proper to introduce the dogs to one another and give them the opportunity to get acquainted before the mating time arrived. They felt that the introduction should take place at a neutral site, so they accepted Madeline's offer to use her den.

On the appointed day, the women gathered to witness the introduction. At the sight of Babette, Beau went bonkers, while she shunned him. When he couldn't caress her, he tried to impress her with his repertoire of tricks, including the ones I thought I had broken him of. When that didn't work, he started running tight circles around the pool table. He ran faster and faster, stopped and upchucked, and fell to the floor, completely exhausted, as the women hysterically applauded his efforts. Afterwards, he staggered home and spent most of the rest of the day sleeping.

Eventually they mated, and Beau sired four beautiful poodles. Madeline got one for hosting the introduction; Arlene kept one and named her Cheri, and she dispersed the others within her family. Beau became a legend in the neighborhood.

Dodo decided to reward him for his accomplishment and took him to the pet shop for a grooming. Upon their return, he reluctantly came into the house and tried to hide behind her. I could see why, for all of his gray hair was gone except for puffs around his ankles and the tip of his tail, and he had a bow atop his head to match the blue polish on his nails. I said it looked like he had been punished.

For the next several days, until he licked or chewed off the nail polish, he spent most of the time hiding behind a sofa or in the garage.

* * * * *

While living at our new home, we continued and really enjoyed our close family relationships. We would spend our two-week vacation at the lake, visit with Dodo's family in Connecticut, and visit my parents upstate. Once we had more room and Dad had retired, my parents would visit us at Thanksgiving, Easter, and, occasionally, Mother's Day. Dad loved sports, so we took him to see a Phillies divisional championship game and an MLB All Star game, where he rooted for Yankee catcher Thurman Munson, who subsequently died in a private plane crash.

* * * * *

Within our neighborhood, there were confirmation, bar mitzvah, and graduation gatherings as well as milestone birthdays and anniversaries. We and one other older couple, as well as about six other, younger couples, became very social with each other. We would hold picnics, swimming pool parties, and clambakes, where Buzz, our former WWII big bomber pilot turned restaurant manager, would prepare and steam individual mesh bags containing clams, corn, and assorted vegetables, while we would grill the various meats.

We would hold Halloween parties and, at one party, we all arrived individually, including the hosts, totally encased in a mask and our handmade or scrounged costumes. We took a seat in the circle of chairs in Madeline and Jack's living room. We sat there mum, trying to further conceal our identities, while our costumed bodies were shaking and our eyes were tear-filled from trying to contain our recognizable laughter at the sight of each new arrival.

A middle-aged neighborhood couple, who was slightly reclusive, and the wife of whom was somewhat critically outspoken, thought it might be fun, and accepted our invite to the party. There were only a few of us seated when they arrived, wearing only eye masks and casual clothes. The woman said hello and asked us if there were any special seating arrangement. Of course we stayed mum and overheard her whisper to her husband, "These people are rude and ignoring us; maybe we should leave." As each new person arrived, she would whisper, "This is eerie; we don't know who these people are, and I'm getting scared."

Dodo was the last one to arrive, and she came dressed as the hunchback of Notre Dame. She was clad in my really old, animal bloodstained, woolen hunting outfit and my oversized boots. Her whole head was encased in a really ugly, elongated, and droopy pointed nose, old hag witch type mask. She dragged her foot as she used my old shotgun as a crutch.

A number of things happened simultaneously. I turned on my concealed mini tape player with a continuous loop of hysterical laughter; Dodo fell to the floor laughing; one of the guests, who always experienced a sudden urge to urinate when enjoying a hardy laugh, jumped up and hit me on the head as she exclaimed, "Damn you, Breezy, I know it's you, and now you've made me have to run to the bathroom." The other woman jumped up and pulled her husband's hand, while shouting, "They're crazy; we're outta here!" as they hurriedly left. They avoided us for quite a while thereafter.

After being doubled over with laughter, we slowly regained our composure. We removed our outer costumes and our masks, disclosing our identities which were virtually already known. All of us, that is, except for one person. Only by the process of elimination did we realize that, it was Al, a slightly shorter and younger member of our group. His homemade costume was great. He had on a long homemade stove pipe topper that made him stoop under the door frames. It sat on his shoulders was secured to his suspenders, and had tiny slits that he could see through. At its base, he had drawn a face on his white shirt, and below that he had attached his young son's clip-on tie. He walked with mini steps that gave you the impression that he was a midget, but the length and height of the topper made you think otherwise.

On Halloween night, Al wore his costume as he walked up and down both sides of the street, to the delight of the trick or treaters. That night, Dodo was traversing the sidewalks in her costume, but without the shot gun. At the sight of her, the older trick or treaters tried to avoid her. The young ones started screaming or crying while grasping their mothers, a few of whom were getting scared and crossing the street to avoid her. Soon there came a murmur that one or two women from the far end of the street, were contemplating alerting the police to an adult weirdo prowling the neighborhood. Soon, Dodo scurried home, just in case they did call the police.

* * * * *

We had a great group of really good friends, and we seldom missed an opportunity to have fun together. Early on the evening of December 24, they dropped in to share cake and ice cream and wish Dodo a happy birthday. One year they had all left, except for Les, Jack, and his wife, Madeline. As she was leaving to put their two young daughters to bed, she asked Jack to come home soon to help her assemble gifts and erect and decorate their tree, which they traditionally did on Christmas Eve. He assured her that he would.

As Jack and Les were leaving, Les looked up at the star-filled sky and said, "It's a beautiful night; I'll get my guitar and we can go caroling." I said, "Great idea," and shocked them when I added that I would get my accordion out of the attic. Dodo said, "Let me get my jacket," and Jack, midway down the driveway, said, "I've got to see and hear this, cause I don't believe you guys can even sing, never mind play instruments." The four of us proceeded next door to the home of our oldest neighbors. They enjoyed our carols, and invited us in to share some homemade wine. We accepted their offer. They thought caroling was a lovely idea and joined us.

The pattern was the same at each home we visited that night. As it got late, we were all exhibiting an outer glow, especially Jack, and were disbanding and wishing one another a Merry Christmas. Jack spoke up and said, "Wait a minute, guys, we didn't stop at my home and sing for Madeline, and she'll be disappointed if we don't." We reminded him that he still had to put up and decorate the tree, but he pleaded, and we relented. Madeline took one look at a now smiling and happily singing Jack, whose voice drowned ours out, and said to us "Look at him; what have you done to him? Once again, I have to do the tree by myself." She interlaced these words a variety of x-rated words. We all went in, sat her down and put up the tree. The women decorated it. By that time Madeline was now smiling, and Jack was asleep and snoring on the couch.

* * * * *

Les and his wife arrived from their hometown in Maryland. He had an outgoing, congenial personality and had an electronic engineering degree. He was an executive at a local electronic manufacturing company. Madeline and Jack were locals who had arrived from a nearby community. They had family and friends residing locally. They were a warmhearted, hard working couple whose door was always open. They offered a helping hand to their families and friends. Jack was a hands-on co-owner of an industrial construction company and was extremely capable in all phases of construction.

They became our really close friends, and we, in essence, became their older sister and brother. We occasionally went out for dinner or a night of bowling, and the women would usually share daily coffee breaks. We men would share cold beer breaks or engage in competitive fun games of basketball or tennis at our local school courts. Most often, however, we were involved in spirited games of pool in Jack's den and were not above pulling silly pranks on one another.

As we returned from our summer vacation one year, our daughters expressed surprise and concern as we all noticed the "for sale" sign on our front lawn. As we were disembarking, our friends were sprawled out on Jack's lawn, laughing and welcoming us home. My suspicion that it was my turn to be pranked was confirmed when I found my house key didn't fit the front or back door. I returned to the front of the house as the group raised their drinks and waved and shouted, "Welcome home!" As I unlocked and opened the garage door, I waved and said, "It's great to be home," as they pummeled Jack for forgetting to change that lock.

CHAPTER NINETEEN
OUR NEW HOME

(Section B)

While living in our new home, our daughters grew rapidly before our eyes. They were doing excellently academically and were participating in extracurricular activities. In 1974, Donna graduated from our local Pennsbury High School in a class of slightly over 1,200 students and was inducted into the National Honor Society. She participated in the basketball and field hockey programs and, in the latter, she made varsity team in her junior year. Diane finished her freshman year and, at the beginning of that year, along with her neighborhood friend, Terri, was selected to and carried the high school marching band banner. They led the 275-member band in parades, sporting events, and competitions. They had earned that honor by developing their marching skills the previous summer marching up and down our street, carrying a banner they had made from scrap wood and bed sheets. They were followed by a marching group of younger kids that they enticed or cajoled into joining them, including Janet, who had just finished fifth grade.

* * * * *

On October 7, 1975, Dodo and I celebrated our 25th wedding anniversary. It was a relatively low key celebration, since I had just been discharged from the hospital the day before. I had been there recuperating, for about 6 days, from surgery wherein my healthy gallbladder had been removed because of a large floating stone that impaired its function. The surgeon had a great sense of humor and gave me the stone in a bottle of formaldehyde to give to Dodo as my personal gift commemorating our milestone anniversary.

Later that night, as we were sharing refreshments with a few of our neighborhood friends, Dodo proudly and humorously displayed the large black stone. She went on to say that she cherished and would preserve this stone of love. Word of the gift soon spread throughout the neighborhood, and a couple of women, whose same anniversary was approaching, began dropping hints to their husbands, embellishing and touting my generosity.

The highlight of our celebration was sharing our dinner and cake with our three daughters, ages 19, 15, and 11. As we blew out the candles, they gave us a gift certificate, for a ten-day group tour of the Hawaiian Islands. Donna facilitated and made the tour arrangements, and our three daughters and my parents contributed financially. We were elated with this gift, for we both loved Hawaiian music and enjoyed movies and TV programs that depicted the island's beauty and culture, which we would now experience firsthand.

Most of all, we were looking forward to a tour of Pearl Harbor. We were a couple weeks shy of our 13th birthdays that fateful day in December 1941 when that sneak attack triggered our country's entry into WWII. But still etched in our mind, these many years later, were the pictures and newsreel reports that showed the carnage and fire that took over two thousand military lives.

We departed on our group tour in late January 1976. Some 12 hours later, we landed at Honolulu on the Island of Oahu, to a beautiful, warm, aloha greeting. Later, as we entered our hotel room, we found a gift-wrapped bottle of champagne and a container of macadamia nuts with an attached note. It read, "Welcome to Hawaii; Happy 25th." It was from my mother's younger sister, Fran, and her husband, John, with whom we had a very close relationship. Later, when we contacted and thanked them, they expressed hope that we felt as happy as they did when their children did the same for them, since they had celebrated their anniversary in Hawaii.

For the next few days, we were typical tourists. We sunned on the sand on Waikiki Beach, joined a crew paddling an outrigger canoe off shore, where we were drenched by the waves, and rode the crest of a wave swiftly back to shore. We toured the pineapple farms and stopped at the North Shore, the site of some of the best surfing waves in the world. And we visited and toured the Polynesian Village," where we learned the peculiarities of the five Polynesian cultures and watched a flotilla of rafts drift by on a canal, with the occupants wearing appropriate garb while demonstrating the traits and rhythms of the various cultures.

In the evenings, we saw some beautiful sunsets, where the sun appeared as a huge fireball as it slowly set over the ocean horizon; took in a dinner show that featured excellent native talent; and sat on mats enjoying a luau on a sandy beach, under the stars and palm trees, surrounded by flaming torches flickering in the ocean breeze while sipping our chi-chis and mai-tais.

Our most solemn event was the day we went on the Pearl Harbor naval tour. As our naval launch left the dock, the excellent young naval tour guide described the chronology of that fateful day's events. He pointed to the mountains and adjacent valleys through which the waves of Japanese planes had flown in undetected; the path they flew while strafing and bombing the shipyard and the ships moored, some in clusters, at the various docks; the carnage and loss of lives that resulted; and the heroism of the survivors, as they risked their own lives while rescuing their injured and oil-covered comrades from the blazing ships and flaming waters.

At our last stop on the tour, we boarded the floating, simplistic, yet powerfully emotional, *Arizona Memorial*. The walls were adorned with pictures of that day's carnage and a roster of the seamen that were entombed in the sunken ship below us. There was many a tear shed by the tourists as we solemnly and respectfully dropped leis and individual flowers in the water, while periodically a bubble of oil popped up to the surface.

We flew over to the big island of Hawaii on the last leg of our tour and landed at the fishing town of Kono. Our beachfront hotel was adjacent to an old native church, and on the other side of the hotel there was a large lava field and the renowned Black Sand Beach. As we were returning from the beach on our first day at our new location, Dodo slipped on a lava rock, severely spraining her ankle. The doctor placed her on crutches for the remaining few days of our trip. The next day, we joined our group for a tour of the Mauna Lea Volcano region, but instead of boarding the tour buses, we were provided private limousine service.

On the last full day of our tour of Hawaii, we transferred to the town of Hilo. Our next day, our departure point had, decades earlier, had been devastated by a tsunami. Here again we were transferred in a private limo, and the ride included an extensive tour of the island. At the Hilo airport, we were provided wheelchair service. As our group was climbing up the long stairway to the 747's front cabin door, we were raised to the back door aboard a platform on an elevator truck, while our traveling companions were giving Dodo a thumb's up.

We did not tell our daughters about Dodo's injury, and as they were waiting to greet us at the Philadelphia Airport, they noticed a wheelchair being wheeled out the passageway to our plane and said, "I bet something happened to Mom." As I wheeled Dodo into the waiting area, she was smiling and waving her crutches at them, while they were roaring and telling each other, "I told you it was for Mom." For a long time afterwards, we cherished and mentally relived that trip, especially for the solemn and joyous memories it generated. Periodically we would wear our Hawaiian shirts, listen to the Hawaiian music albums, and look at the travel pictures that we brought back, as a way of rekindling those memories.

* * * * *

In the summer of 1976, our home life and my work environment were running smoothly. Donna had completed her second year at our community college and was now enrolled at a nearby 4-year college in Trenton, New Jersey, to complete her college degree. Diane completed her junior year at our high school and her first year as the co-drum majorette of the marching band. Janet finished seventh grade and, along with her various activities, became my fishing buddy and Dodo's little helper, as she began taking a delight in cooking.

Prior to the start of the new school year, our teachers declared a strike. The football team coaching staff, to the distaste of the teachers and their union leaders, crossed the picket lines and continued the practices. They said it was their way of showing commitment and respect to the team, especially the seniors, who had committed to and worked so hard to make the program a success. Without supervision, but with strong determination, the band members continued to practice their upcoming patriotic program. Our local newspaper ran a feature article on the band practicing, including a picture of Diane and her co-partner leading the band through their hours of daily practice.

At the season opening game, on a beautiful Saturday afternoon, the football team, accompanied by the coaching staff, ran onto the field. Simultaneously, Diane and her co-partner led the 275-member marching band, that had been denied access to their uniforms, into the stadium in perfect unison, wearing sneakers, dungarees, t-shirts, baseball caps, and their band member jackets, blaring the school fight song, *Hail To The Falcons*. The crowd rose and, for an extended time, stood stomping, yelling, and applauding in a rousing display of support to the participants on the field. The team had a really good season, and the band had a minute or two of national exposure when they performed their patriotic routine at a nationally televised Philadelphia Eagles game.

* * * * *

In the summer of 1976, in the midst of our happy home and work environment, the Department of Defense confirmed previous rumors and announced that Frankford Arsenal would be closed on September 30, 1977, as a projected cost-saving measure. They went on to say that several of the Arsenal elements would be eliminated while others, along with associated personnel, would be transferred to Picatinny Arsenal in Northern New Jersey some 70 miles away.

I was appointed to a task group and, over the next few months, we assembled data and produced documentation for our local congressmen to present at congressional hearings on the closure.

The data we assembled not only disputed the cost-saving claim made by the Department of Defense, but it also showed that the economic loss to the greater Philadelphia and southern New Jersey area would dwarf any estimated cost savings.

We developed data that showed that the Department of Defense would suffer a severe loss of a workforce of well over 1,000 highly-trained technical personnel, most of them WWII veterans. They were at their peak in experience and expertise and were actively working in the development and production fields of high priority military equipment needed by the Army. The people in this group formed most of the core of our management structure along with project leader and senior technician positions.

Our contention was the result of a survey we had done wherein we found that all of the 55 and older age group, with at least 30 years of service, were planning to reject the job relocation offer and, rather than uproot their families, would in fact retire, since they met all of the minimum eligibility retirement requirements. In the 50 and older age group, with at least 25 years of service, we found that most of them refused to uproot their families, would reject the job relocation offer, and would accept an early retirement package being offered by the government, albeit at a slightly reduced retirement annuity. Finally, we contended that, for a long time to come, but, more importantly, in the short term, the receiving agency would be unable to effectively or efficiently replace the skilled work pool loss, and top military programs currently underway would suffer severe setbacks in time and cost.

The year 1976 was a Presidential election year. In mid-October, the Democratic Party's candidate for Vice President, Walter Mondale, was briefed on the Arsenal closure during a campaign visit to the area, and he publicly promised that if he and Presidential nominee, Jimmy Carter, were elected, they would stop the Arsenal closure. They won decidedly in Philadelphia and won the national election, and our spirits were cautiously raised.

CHAPTER TWENTY
LIFE CHANGES

Within a couple of months of the inauguration of the new President and Vice President in January of 1977, it became apparent that, in spite of our local congressional efforts, the new administration was ignoring their previous promise and the Arsenal closure was proceeding on schedule. By spring, many younger employees were leaving for other local jobs; retirements began and would soon occur in droves, and critical program progress was rapidly decreasing and would soon virtually come to a halt.

(Note: in 1980, the new administration was defeated by Ronald Reagan in their re-election bid.)

I found myself in a difficult situation in that I had the minimum 25 years of service requirement to receive the one time early retirement package being offered, but I was 15 months shy of the minimum 50-year age requirement. Since civil service job opportunities in the local area were rarely available at my grade level, I was left with two basic options, either accept or reject a job transfer offer, a decision I would have to make by my transfer date, which was scheduled for late September 1977.

Over time, Dodo and I extensively discussed our options. Each time that we did, we agreed that accepting the job offer was our best option. It would give our family financial stability for the next 6 years, and I could then retire at age 55 with a comfortable retirement annuity. Its main drawback was that we would most likely have to uproot our family.

We considered rejecting the transfer, but that essentially meant starting anew. If I was fortunate enough to find a job in the local private industry, at my income level and age, I would have work until age 60, which was the age at which I would qualify for my government pension, but at a significantly reduced annuity level.

In June 1977, Donna completed her junior year at a local college, and Diane graduated our high school as a member of the National Honor Society, and was preparing to depart to college in August. Janet finished 8th grade and was looking forward to her freshman year at our high school. She had become my fishing buddy and a die-hard Phillies fan after attending the 1976 All Star game in Philadelphia, which prompted us to purchase a 3-seat, sixteen game season ticket plan that we were now enjoying.

That month, Dodo, Janet, and I went on a one-week house hunting trip to northern New Jersey. We went on this trip knowing deep down that the trauma of uprooting and moving our family was an option, but would only be given serious consideration if we could see that such a move would demonstrably and significantly elevate our family lifestyle and comfort, since staying put and commuting was always an option.

We found some equivalent areas in New Jersey, but the few available homes and their associated taxes were well beyond what we could afford. We found a couple of affordable homes, in much older towns, but they were located in less than desirable neighborhoods and school systems.

We skipped on over to the Stroudsburg area in northeast Pennsylvania for a look-see. This was an attractive area located in the rolling foothills of the nearby Pocono Mountains with a stable population and, thus, very few homes for sale. New home developments were beginning in rural pockets in the area and were projecting 15 or so homes to be built in a spacious cluster, a mile or more outside town. These were attractive sites and certainly much more affordable than the northern Jersey area, and many of the younger transferees chose these sites to permanently relocate their families. It still required a minimum 45-minute daily commute each way, and the area experienced long and often severe winter weather conditions.

We returned from that visit more convinced that commuting, which would maintain our family's stability, comfort, and security at our current residence, was our best option. We spent the rest of the summer relaxed, insofar as we did not have to face the trauma of uprooting and moving.

* * * * *

At work, it was a different matter. Around the beginning of July, units of the Arsenal and the relatively small group of employees who accepted the transfer offer, began moving to the new agency. The rest of that unit's employees retired or accepted severance packages based on years of service. This pattern repeated every few weeks as additional units moved to the new agency per the preset schedule. As the Arsenal productivity was rapidly deteriorating and coming to a halt, people like me who were still at the Arsenal, including imminent retirees, were now going through all of our files and desks, identifying, separating, and boxing documents to be transferred to the new agency.

I was also concentrating on and developing a commuting plan. All of the carpools being formed were sufficiently outside my locale to be an option. A local friend, whose family also remained in our area, transferred to the new agency in the first wave. He was sharing an apartment with a friend of ours who was awaiting completion of his new home, which was scheduled to be finished at the end of November. We agreed that I would move in at that time.

During the interim, I arranged to rent a room in a wonderful elderly couple's home.

* * * * *

In the latter half of September 1997, I reported to Picattiny Arsenal in the last transfer wave, and I was directed to my new work site. As I walked the sidewalk, to the one story, elongated wooden WWII building, I had a misstep while evading the droppings, strewn all up and down the walk, by a nearby feeding and fraternizing flock of ducks. As I was cleaning my shoe and murmuring expletives, I looked around and rhetorically asked myself if this was the environment that I wanted to work in for the next 6 years. Little did I know that this event would be the high point of roughly my first 18 months of employment at the newly structured command.

I was assigned to the fire control engineering group as a senior engineering technician, and after a week or so of housekeeping activities, we settled in. I knew a few people in the group, but I especially knew and was friendly with George, a general engineer, whom I had met some 15 years earlier as we worked together on the conceptual automatic diagnostic program and occasionally thereafter on some other programs. He was designated the command development projection officer (DPO) for the M60A3 tank fire control system. He was responsible for managing, overseeing, and assessing the performance of the various command direct rates involved in the program, and he appointed me as his assistant DPO.

The fire control system consisted of a laser range finder and a ballistic computer system. Mechanical and optical components were tightly packaged into two cast modules. The system was developed to be installed in the latest Army tank version to provide greater fire power accuracy.

Frankford Arsenal awarded the development and the initial follow-up production contracts to a defense company on the West Coast, with the initial production deliveries scheduled to begin in late 1977. They also awarded a production contract to a second source to establish a competitive environment for future fiscal year buys. Deliveries were to begin in the latter part of 1978.

During the final several months of the Arsenal closure, and at a critical point in the contract, all the key government technical personnel working on the program were retiring, or leaving for other local employment opportunities, rather than relocating to the new command. We began hearing rumors that the production program was in trouble. As we took on the program management responsibilities at our new command, we formed a cadre team of representatives from the various involved parties. Only a couple of the team members had any knowledge of the program, and that knowledge was limited at best.

In response to our request for a status report, the lead contractor informed us that he was experiencing production problems, the extent of which were being determined and analyzed, and that the initial deliveries, scheduled to begin the next month, would be delayed by a minimum of six months. The next Sunday, George and I flew out to the West Coast, spent the next three days at the contractor's facility evaluating the problems, took the red eye flight back to the East Coast to spend Thanksgiving Day with our families, and proceeded to our command location to brief our commanding major general. He as a colonel was the project officer who led the effort and oversaw the closure of the Arsenal, which led to his promotion to the two star level.

George informed the general that the lead contractor was experiencing numerous production and testing problems and that the root cause was an unstable technical data package (TDP). The follow-up production contractor was working with the same TDP, and could be expected to experience similar production delays pending stabilization of the TDP, and the tank project manager would be forced to store and delay the fielding of a significant number of incomplete tanks that would be awaiting delivery of the fire control systems.

The TDP was essentially a microfilm package that contained all of the drawings, specifications, and other pertinent data that defined the item to be built. It also included the production, assembly, and testing processes that were to be used to ensure government acceptance of the hardware.

The TDP was produced by the lead contractor during the development phase, and in his initial production contract he had a line item requirement to scrub the TDP and certify adequacy and accuracy to accommodate mass production techniques in the production of identically configured operational units. Any changes or corrections to the TDP were to be submitted as engineering change proposals (ECP) to the government for review and approval, before incorporation into the TDP and production process.

It was important that the lead contractor undertake the TDP scrubbing effort early on, particularly before beginning the in-house manufacturing of or placing of purchase orders for items with long lead times. Otherwise, major errors in the TDP would not necessarily be detected until months later, during the initial assembly and testing phase. Depending on the severity of the corrective actions required, severe production and delivery delays could be experienced, and that was the situation we were facing.

In 1978, we were working long hours in a crisis mode that at times was demoralizing and frustrating. We were receiving ECPs to correct errors in the TDP from the lead contractor at an average rate approaching 100 per month, which further contributed to production delays. After their approval, the ECPs were incorporated into the follow-up producer's TDP. These additions were creating delays in his production schedule. Meanwhile, incomplete tanks were beginning to be stored, and their quantities increased with every additional month's production slippages.

In view of the volume of ECPs being received and processed within the command established procedure, wherein the ECP was evaluated by the involved parties and eventually approved by a configuration control board that met one day a week, it was taking an average 30 calendar days to process an ECP. We hired two retirees who had previously been key technical people on the program as consultants to help us expedite the technical evaluation of the ECPs.

George requested the authority to establish a dedicated team of representatives along with configuration control board authorities to expedite the processing of ECPs and to reduce the time to an average of 15 calendar days. The general noted the request and told us to proceed with the utmost urgency but within the established command processing procedures.

We were also heavily involved in other program-related activities. We were frequently in travel mode, providing assistance or conducting program reviews at our contractor facilities and attending reviews at the tank project manager's office at the tank command in Detroit. We were negotiating new split fiscal year buys with our contractors, when, late one evening, as we finally and successfully completed several days of negotiations, we exited the building to the sound and sight of nearby fireworks. Someone asked, "What's the occasion?" and the reply came "It's the Fourth of July."

I was tasked with preparing a weekly program status report for our commander's submission to his four-star boss in D.C. The report primarily addressed the top technical problems that were hindering production progress and the progress being made in their resolution. The bottom line, however, was that the initial production was falling increasingly behind schedule and incomplete tanks were now being stored in increasing quantities.

The year 1979 began as a replica of the previous year, but we were soon seeing the beginning of some notable progress. Our ECP receipts rate dropped to an average of 80 per month. We approved a sufficient quantity of critical ECPs, and the lead contractor implemented the required corrective actions into the production hardware and processes, to the point that, in March, the randomly selected systems of the first month's production quantity passed the first article critical environments test phase, and we began accepting their produced systems, some 15 months behind the original schedule.

Our four-star commander at the Pentagon established an independent commission to evaluate the program status and to recommend corrective or additional actions. They visited the involved agencies and interviewed the appropriate personnel. They spent extensive time interviewing George and me, our technical group, and personnel from other participating directorates and reviewed our work process and command wide procedures. During the exit meeting, they commended us on our work ethic and product and opined that command wide we were understaffed and too decentralized and that their report would contain appropriate recommendations.

* * * * *

About the end of 1979, a new two-star major general took over our command responsibilities. George and I met with him, and we had a fairly detailed discussion regarding our command wide program tasks, since he had received an overview of the program and the commission's effort preceding his arrival. As we formulated an initial overview action plan, his calm, confident, perceptive, and notably down-to-earth humane persona became evident and increased over time.

By early January 1980, the general had authorized and chartered a dedicated 46-member team to intensively manage the entire program under George's leadership, and I was designated the assistant. The General met with our newly assembled team, thanked us for our willingness and desire to contribute to this critical program, expressed his total support, encouraged the generation of innovative actions to accelerate the program's progress, and requested our maximum effort, but not to the point where it would deteriorate our health or families.

George concentrated his efforts on working with our technical team segments and their very active and competent group leaders. He had me coordinate the activities of all of the team segments, particularly as those elements contributed to the production and delivery of hardware by both contractors, and I defined the overall team critical tasks, and tracked and reported on our progress. Our team elements included engineering, procurement, production, product, assurance, financial management, and configuration management, which included our own configuration review board.

The general accompanied us to a management review at both of our contractor facilities, and in his remarks he basically delivered the message that he had given our team. His expressed attention to the program and presence at the meeting was reflected by the attending corporate CEOs, and they announced the formation of their own dedicated teams.

Among the many actions underway were several actions that accelerated hardware production. We assigned two technicians, with diverse backgrounds and experience, to each of the contractor's facilities to provide onsite assistance. They possessed the authority to approve certain actions; we established a data fax line with both contractors wherein we transmitted appropriate action documents, including ECPs, and began processing each ECP within 15 calendar days.

As a result of the extensive efforts underway, our lead contractor soon reached a sustainable maximum monthly production rate, and our follow-up contractor delivered his initial systems and was in the build-up phase to reach his maximum monthly rates.

By June 1980, some six months after the formation of the dedicated teams, and a couple months ahead of our earlier projection, our system deliveries were slightly ahead of the program requirements on a cumulative basis, but it was not yet time to celebrate. The program would soon enter a phase wherein the monthly hardware requirements would rapidly increase to accommodate full-scale tank production rates and the required allocation of hardware to other program elements. Our main effort now was to keep our delivery posture positive.

With deliveries now underway from both contractors, and with input from them and our on-site representatives,

I was able to project, with reasonable confidence, attainable monthly delivery rates for the next 12 months. The tank project office furnished us with a spread sheet that contained all of the various monthly requirements covering the same period. Previously, I had manually tracked, analyzed, and projected deliveries and our hardware delivery posture on a 1- to 2-month basis. Doing it for a 12-month period, with monthly updates, could be a little tedious.

While discussing the task I was undertaking with Del, our computer specialist, he proffered to generate a computer program that would include the math and analysis I was seeking. He eventually did a computer run, and the printed output contained the data I needed, particularly the CUM deliveries vs. requirements, and the Delta.

In this case, the data showed that our projected CUM deliveries would exceed the RQMTS in each of the 12 months. As the CUM requirements remained firm, our contractor deliveries consistently met or at times exceeded the projections. When the latter occurred, Del input the one, or at most two, new numbers, and the output reflected the more positive downstream ripple effect. What a fantastic time-saving analytical tool, considering that computer technology capability was in its infancy!

As we progressed into 1981, all of our team actions were completed and the recurring ones were being completed on schedule. We completed the actions recommended by the independent commission, accepted the certified TDP that contained the slightly more than 3,000 approved ECPs, and awarded two additional fiscal year buys totaling $162 million after an updated analysis. We also maintained a schedule that would keep the system's delivery posture positive for the next two years.

In March, the fire control program was described as sound and ready to transfer to the readiness command in Illinois. They had primary program responsibility for the full deployment and field maintenance support and training. I had the responsibility of developing and coordinating the plan with the readiness command. Commanders approved the plan, the acquired actions were completed and the program management responsibility was transitioned on June 30 as scheduled.

At the request of our commander, I prepared and he transmitted to his four-star boss in Washington, a comprehensive final program progress report that included the program status and our team's and contractors' accomplishments. We described the program as technically and administratively sound with no major obstacles to impede either contractor's continued delivery and noted that we were reducing our team strength to a level needed to provide technical support to the readiness command. Now was the time to celebrate.

In celebration, we held a team on-post golf outing, and were joined by our general. We also invited representatives from the other participating agencies. That day, it didn't matter who you were, what rank you were, or what golfing talent you had, the main thing was that everybody had fun. That spirit extended to the awards ceremony buffet, at which the general remarked, "This team works hard and knows how to have fun."

At an awards night buffet party for the entire team and spouses, the general, in his remarks, thanked the team for its efforts and accomplishments, and our family members for their support for us. He posed for a picture with each member as he presented a Department of Army official commendation for a special act and a monetary award. On the way to the party, knowing we'd be seated at his table, Dodo asked if there was any special protocol to be observed. I told her "No, just be yourself." They had some fun conversations, since he was interested in her background and upbringing. Later, Dodo said, "I see why you like and respect him; he's a good, down-to-earth person and is as easy to converse with as are our friends."

In early 1980, when the general came on board and authorized the dedicated team effort, I had the responsibility to track and report on the overall program and, more specifically, the hardware delivery status. The reporting was accomplished via a weekly program progress letter that I prepared and delivered to the general on Friday afternoons for his signature and forwarding to his boss. He initially gave me his guidelines that the one-page letter should address our major tasks with basic facts that didn't require analysis or contain unnecessary details. He routinely signed the letters and, on rare occasions, he would change or add a word or two or add a comment.

During the weekly interactions, we had an appropriate, respectful relationship, but it also developed into a warm, comfortable, and personal one, often sprinkled with humor. Exiting our first meeting with the general, George remarked, "You two really hit it off like two old friends. It was nice to observe and it's unique in military protocol and your substantively lower rank." He was referring to a discussion early in the meeting.

As a way to get to know each other, the general had expressed interest in our background, families, and whether we had relocated or were commuters. He told us that he was a native of south central Pennsylvania and had attended and graduated from Lebanon Valley College in that area in the late 1940s. I told him that I was a native of a northeast Pennsylvania coal mining town and had attended and graduated from the University of Scranton in that area, also in the 1940s. As a member of the basketball team, I had played in home and away games against his alma mater, and I recalled the names of their outstanding player and the twin brothers on their team. He looked a little surprised and said, "John, you've just named three of my best friends in college." Our discussion expanded as we sought other similarities.

After about a month or so, I delivered the letter a little later than usual that Friday afternoon. As the general signed it, he commented, "John, you should be home in Pennsylvania by now, or at least on the way. I'm sure your wife is anxiously awaiting your arrival. Hereafter bring me the letter on Thursdays." During these weekly interactions, he would often ask how Dodo was coping with my weeknight absences, how our daughters were doing, and if there were exciting events in their lives.

The day of our golf outing, while practicing on the putting green, the General felt he'd shoot a "hot" round and proposed that we have a side bet, with the winner to get his choice of a top shelf drink. We agreed on a series of plus and minus points. Later we were at the bar laughing as we analyzed and tallied each other's points and he conceded and ordered my drink.

At the commendation awards family night, as we were shaking hands as he presented my commendation, under his breath and with a sly look he asked, "By the way John, how many cokes did you win from Murray?" I was momentarily taken aback, as I had no idea that he knew about the bet and laughingly replied, "Nine." He cocked his head and had a burst of laughter at the moment that our formal picture was taken. Dodo later asked what the laughing was all about.

I told her that earlier in the year, a colonel whose first name was Murray had become our new directorate commander and had to initial the weekly letter. The first week that we met, he asked for and I gave him the details on various aspects of the program. He felt that many of the details should be included in the letter, and I felt that the general would not sign a letter containing such details. After a respectful back and forth, he asked if I was willing to bet a coke that the general would sign the letter as written. I agreed to the bet, and he asked that I leave him a message regarding the outcome. Later, I left him the message, "You owe John a coke." The routine was the same for the next 8 weeks, and the following week Murray initialed the letter and said, "Mo more bets."

Dodo was shaking her head in disbelief as she said, "You've got to be kidding me, you two were up there yakking it up like two kids, oblivious to us, all over a silly bet." Then she added, "You two are alike and both of you are crazy."

* * * * *

Up through the summer of 1977, our family was typical and relatively stable. Routinely there were the five of us enjoying our weeknight and weekend dinners together and discussing the day's activities. Dramatically, that routine changed as I transferred to the new command and commuted primarily on weekends.

Diane moved to Bethlehem, Pennsylvania, to attend a two-year, full-time college program. She simultaneously obtained a job in that area working as a restaurant waitress, primarily on weekends, and her visits home were occasional and short.

Donna was in her senior year at a nearby college, with a short daily commute, and also worked as a waitress at a pub near the college.

On weekends, we could count on Dodo, Janet, and me at the dinner table. We were occasionally joined by Donna or Diane, as their schedules permitted. During the week it was routinely Dodo and Janet, who was in her high school freshmen year. They both put forth fantastic effort in assuming the household and even handyman chores that I usually did in order to free up my weekends at home. They formed a very close bond, as Janet became very interested in cooking and quilting, and Dodo was happy to pass on these traits to Janet. In fact, she welcomed and encouraged Janet's participation in both.

In spite of our diversified schedules, we made sure we set aside time to be together during the holidays, extended family visits, and memorable family events. With the girls' summer calendar filled, as was the Murphy kids', our joint summer vacations came to an end. We continued visiting with Dodo's family at Christmas and sporadically during the year. We continued visiting my parents over the Christmas holiday, and they visited with us at Thanksgiving, Easter, and Mother's Day.

It was also a time that we enjoyed a serious of memorable family events. In 1978, Donna graduated college with a B.A. in education and began substitute teaching in a local school district. That December, we celebrated our 50th birthdays, and the girls presented us with a gift certificate for a five-day, all-expenses-paid trip to the Bahamas. In December 1979, Diane completed her two-year college program as a radiological technician, returned home and began working at a local medical center.

For the next two years, the enjoyable trend continued. In 1980, we enjoyed attending the Phillies games. They won their division, and Dodo and I, accompanied by Janet, celebrated our 30th anniversary cheering on the team in the World Series game from our upper deck seats.

In 1981, Janet graduated from high school and began her college freshman year at the nearby Penn State extension campus. Diane moved to the Bethlehem, Pennsylvania, area, where she accepted a position as a radiology technician at Lehigh Valley Trauma Center. In August, Donna got married, and her sisters were bridesmaids. It was a beautiful church ceremony, and a large gala reception filled the night with fun.

CHAPTER TWENTY-ONE

UNTIL WE MEET AGAIN...

As we were celebrating New Year's Eve with our friends and welcoming in the year 1982, Dodo and I reminisced about the previous year's events. We recognized that our family was entering a new phase, one of natural evolution, as your children move out to make their own mark. We were pleased that Donna and Diane had their college degrees and that Janet was started on hers. As we toasted each other, I remarked that the worst was over and that within two years I would be retired, and I told Dodo that she would have to put up with me full time. She hugged me as she responded, "I'm looking forward to it; I've missed you all those weeknights." We both agreed that we had made the right decision in keeping our family life stable.

A few weeks into 1982, Dodo began experiencing occasional incidents of lightheadedness. Our family doctor had her undergo a series of tests, and all of the results were normal. In April, Dodo visited our doctor, because she was experiencing soreness in her left shoulder and arm. The doctor conducted extensive EKG tests; all results were normal, and they scheduled her to undergo stress tests the following week.

Three days before the scheduled stress tests, Dodo was hospitalized after passing out at home. While being checked in the emergency unit, she experienced, according to the doctors, two separate mild heart attacks. She was given a nitroglycerin tablet, stabilized, and was admitted in the intensive care unit. For the next two days, the doctors were optimistic, as Dodo seemingly bounced back. She was sitting up, totally alert and relaxed, eating full meals and anxiously looking forward to a release.

In the early morning hours of April 28, 1982, the hospital called and told me that Dodo had taken a turn for the worse and that it would be advisable for the family to immediately come in. Dodo was mentally alert, but under physical stress. We visited with her for a short period as they were preparing for emergency surgery. During the next few hours, we visited the chapel and were immersed in our concerns and praying that God would save her. Later that morning, the doctors met with us in the family room and told us that they had tried their best but that Dodo had died from a massive heart attack at the age of 53.

We were stunned, devastated, and in shock, as were our families and friends, and I found myself sharing one of her earlier feelings that life could be unfair. At the burial, my mother commented, "She was like a daughter to me; I feel like I lost another daughter." I knew I had lost my best friend and realized that never again would I be able to extend my hand to a new acquaintance and say, "Hi, I'm Breezy, and this is my wife, Dodo."

EPILOGUE

This story was originally released chapter by chapter to several family and friends via e-mail. The Acknowledgement and Introduction pages were the e-mail messages that accompanied the first chapter when it was sent. The following is the e-mail message contained when the last chapter was sent on October 7, 2014:

Hello Everyone,

Well the time has come for the release of the last chapter of my Dad's book. He asked me to pass along the following message:

"I thought that it would be real nice to release the final chapter of the Breezy and Dodo story on the day that we would have been celebrating our 64th wedding anniversary. It was an interesting experience documenting our story. At times, it felt like I was opening a lid on a treasure chest of memories.

I hope that you enjoyed the story as much as I enjoyed your comments and recollections. I wish you and yours a wealth of health and happiness. Until we meet again…

Regards,

Breezy."

On a personal note, I would like to thank my Dad for all the time and effort he spent to explain not only who Breezy and Dodo are, but also about our heritage and the history of this country, and not stopping until it was complete, especially during these past couple years. I would also like to thank those who helped him along the way: Aunt Lorraine, Aunt Belle, and Kitty with research of the ancestors, names, dates, and the towns, and Diane, who helped Dad with editing. I learned, laughed, and cried.

Janet

About the Author

John and his future wife, Dorothy, were born to families of Polish immigrants who migrated to northeastern Pennsylvania in the late 1800s and early 1900s for a better life. John was born on the kitchen table in his grandmother's house in Dickson City, Pennsylvania, where he grew up and eventually met Dorothy.

They grew up during the Great Depression and World War II. Upon graduating from Dickson City High School, John attended the University of Scranton on a basketball scholarship and began dating Dorothy. John served in the military from 1952 to 1954, which led to his career working at the Department of the Army.

John and Dorothy were married in 1950 and settled in southeastern Pennsylvania, where they lived, worked, and raised their family. John and Dorothy worked together to achieve the American dream of becoming middle-class Americans.

This biography is John's first literary work. What began as John dictating his life along with that of his wife, the late Dorothy "Dodo" Buza, for his daughters and grandchildren, evolved to include the heritage of the two families, background information on the area where the families settled in Pennsylvania, and a slice of the history of this country.

19947773R00187